FAILURE
The Secret to Success

Robby Slaughter

© 2010 Method Press

Publisher
Method Press / An Imprint of AccelaWork
6100 Keystone, Suite #654
Indianapolis, IN 46220

For further information, please visit www.accelawork.com
or call 1-888-200-9387.

Failure: The Secret to Success
© 2010 Robby Slaughter. All Rights Reserved.

Cover design by Slaughter Development
Photograph by Nicholas Moore. Used with permission courtesy of iStockPhoto.com.

First Printing: 2010

No part of this book may be reproduced or transmitted in any form, or by any means, electrical or mechanical, including photocopying, recording or by any information storage and retrieval system, without the express written permission of the author.

Disclaimer: While the author and publisher have used their best efforts in preparing this book, they make no representations or warranties with regard to accuracy or completeness of this book and specifically disclaim any implied warranties of merchantability or fitness for a particular purpose. The advice and strategies herein may not be appropriate for your situation. This work does not constitute professional services or counsel. Neither the publisher nor the author shall be liable for any loss or damages resulting from the use of this book, including but not limited to special, incidental, consequential or other damages occurred in connection with material presented in this book.

For SB

Acknowledgements

The first and most significant failure in any book occurs on the cover, where the reader is willfully deceived that only one person should receive credit for the work. A long sequence of failures then appears within the section titled "acknowledgements." I shall fail to sufficiently list all of the people who made this book possible, and I shall fail to adequately enumerate their contributions.

Ashley Lee deserves tremendous praise as my editor and tireless supporter of this project. She produced much of the outline, conducted significant research and orchestrated seemingly endless edits and read-throughs. She also uncovered many of the inspiring quotations throughout the book. Ashley also located the amazing image on the front cover and provided significant advice and motivation over many long months.

The rest of the team at AccelaWork also acted as a considerable resource for this book, including content originating from Josh Goldberg's research and tireless, ongoing promotional support from Stephanie Daily.

Much of this book came to life thanks to the constant encouragement of friends and colleagues to continue writing. This includes members of the Indiana Writers Group, especially Kate Chaplin, Debra Kemp, Ellen Tevault, Cheryl Shore, Jamie Carie, Chuck Lasker and Sarah Gott. My old professor Tony Petrosino, as well, always provides great material, commentary and wisdom. I must also thank my many networking circles, from the unflagging support of Rainmakers like Nikki Lewallen, Amy Woodall and Jessica Strom as well as my fellow Geist Overtime board members Eric Marasco, Danielle Rule, Matt Wallpe, Susan Meskis, Kelly Gaskins, Dave McCarty, Betsy Knoke and Joseph Krall. Likewise, my recent membership in Business Networking International has already proven fruitful for this book, as well as the motivating presence of my Business Improvement Council co-founder Hazel Walker.

I also must thank the team at Indy Reads, which has been a long partner in helping to promote our events and provide a gateway to the non-profit community. In particular, these include Kindra Hunckler, Angie Garcia and Travis DiNicola.

In addition to the help of these many people, I must also admit that this book was fueled by the Pike Place Roast of Starbucks #2377 in Broad Ripple, Indiana, and the smiles (and caffeine) offered by Sara, JC, Brian, Vaughan, Kristen, Torrey, Brandon and others.

The loving community at Immaculate Heart of Mary Catholic Church helped to me to recognize the transformative power of sharing our failures with others. These in particular are the men of CRHP 16: Dave Stuhldreher, Mark Graham, Bill Page, Bill Janetta, Dave McGuire, John Cougan, Kenny Crossland, Mike Semler, Bryon Konvolinka and Jac Leonardi. Their faith and confidence in me continues to be evident.

I owe my parents, my brother and my entire extended family a debt of insurmountable gratitude for their many years of love and affection, both as a reader of my words and a source of profound insight. They are unafraid to try and fail, and always willing to lend an ear or a hand.

Most of all, however, I will certainly fail to sufficiently express my thanks to my wife Kathy. This book was produced during the first year of our marriage and will reach shelves before our first anniversary. If anyone deserves to be praised as the secret of my success it is my life partner and best friend.

Table of Contents

Chapter 1: Failure IS an Option 13
The most dangerous phrase in the English language is, "We've always done it this way."

Chapter 2: Before Starting, Try Failing 25
In the simplest terms, failure is the ultimate teacher.

Chapter 3: Great Ways to Fail Better 39
The cliché is right: If you take no risks, there will be no rewards.

Chapter 4: Even More Ways to Fail Better 51
A scholar is one who rejoices in the discovery of their own mistakes.

Chapter 5: A Methodology for Failure 67
Failure is simply the opportunity to begin again, this time more intelligently.

Chapter 6: Failure at Work: Great Failures in Business 85
You might not be doing anything wrong. Rather: The world has changed, and you must change with it.

Chapter 7: Failure is a Perspective, Not a Practice 101
You can have moderate success by copying someone else, but tremendous success requires taking chances.

Chapter 8: Congratulations, You've Failed! Now What? 115
We can only make fantastic advances through many failures.

Chapter 9: Winning by Failing 137
Plan to throw one away, you will anyhow.

Chapter 1

Failure IS an Option

> The most dangerous phrase in the [English] language is, "We've always done it this way."
> –Grace Hopper

What is failure? That seems like an easy question. Failure is screwing up. It is making mistakes. It is stumbling where we intend to walk, falling down where we hoped to climb. Failure is the message: "You're doing it wrong."

Sometimes, failure can be gigantic. Think of the Mitchell Report, which accused eighty-nine Major League Baseball players of using performance-enhancing steroids. That's not just one slugger on one team breaking the rules; it's a player in practically every club in the league.

On the other hand, failures are often minuscule. If we cut ourselves shaving, no one may ever know but us. Failures don't always matter. You might get a bad grade on one assignment, but if you're a good student otherwise it might have a negligible impact on your GPA.

Perhaps the most powerful aspect of the size of failures is how they affect other people. When a little league outfielder fails to catch an easy pop-fly, he may cost his team the game. Losing a game could throw off the whole season or ruin the chances to make the playoffs. Hence the old proverb, "For Want of a Nail:"

> For want of a nail the shoe was lost.
> For want of a shoe the horse was lost.
> For want of a horse the rider was lost.
> For want of a rider the battle was lost.
> For want of a battle the kingdom was lost.
> And all for the want of a horseshoe nail.

The transmission of failure does not always go up the chain. When the Mitchell Report soured baseball and brought so many great players under suspicion, failure was evident on a national scale. How many young sports fans lost their faith in their favorite athletes? How many baseball cards and autographs were thrown away in disgust? Sometimes, the most significant failures by national heroes trickle down to everyday people.

However, failure doesn't always lead to more failure. If you apply for a job but flub the interview, you will fail to get the spot. But you may also make room for another candidate to advance their career. When one team loses a game or an army loses a battle, the opposing side must have been victorious. In the end, your failure may be offset by someone else's success.

Making the wrong decision may clear the way for someone else or it may also demonstrate what **not** to do. Many of the stories that are part of our popular culture are about failure and resolution. In the best-selling book *The Life of Washington* (1809), a story is told about a young George Washington who chopped down a cherry tree because he wanted to use his new hatchet. Even in the mid-1700s, people felt that random deforestation was unwarranted. Yet the story continues that when confronted with the evidence, George Washington did the right thing, exclaiming, "I cannot tell a lie." The mistake of chopping down the tree led to an act of honesty and more importantly, created an invaluable lesson that continues to inspire countless generations.

Perhaps the most powerful aspect of failure is the interplay between failure and success. The story of George Washington certainly has had a positive influence on our culture. Yet at the same time, most historians agree that the author of *The Life of Washington*, Mason Weems, fabricated the entire tale! For nearly two hundred years, students of American history have believed a lie about the first president of our nation. Surely creating and believing in untrue stories is considered failure; especially for those of us gullible enough to entrust our own moral guidance to such tall tales. However, does the lesson of the Washington story outweigh the fact that it is untrue? Is our failure forgiven when we discover we were wrong about some tidbit of American history and correct ourselves?

This is the great question about success and failure. Should we, as human beings, tally up our experiences in life as though our victories and defeats are marks on a scoreboard of our personal worth? If so, every time we accomplish something, we gain points. Every time we screw up, those points vanish. And while the work piles up, the chances to succeed or fail become more overwhelming. Should we even try to keep score? As humorist Bill Watterson once noted, "God put me on this earth to accomplish a certain number of things. Right now I am so far behind that I will never die."

There is an easy way to avoid failure: attempt nothing. This is the route many of us pursue when we encounter a challenging project or a difficult decision. Failure seems like such a black mark on our record that we often try to escape the pangs of error by not taking risks. We sometimes avoid the possibility of screwing up by refusing to venture outside our safety zone.

This strategy does work. If we don't sign up for that committee, we can't be held responsible for any future mistakes. If we don't apply for that premier university, we will not be rejected.

But there is a tragic side effect to insulating ourselves from the possibility of failure. If we refuse to take chances that could lead to major errors we also miss the opportunity for significant wins. You cannot have great success without great failure.

All of this discussion about failure may seem less than encouraging. After all, we can all look back in our lives at the times where we went wrong and feel regret. You may be thinking that you'd rather not revisit those embarrassing memories. If failure is so essential, why is it still so frustrating? Do we really have to be ready to fail again and take on all of the negative consequences of our next disaster?

The answer may not be what you expect. Failure is essential. Failure will continue to be part of your life. Fortunately, by adopting a new perspective on how failure can actually help, you will be able to achieve more. To understand how failure can be the secret to success, we must study failure itself in more detail.

Let's be honest: Not many people like to talk about their failures. If you're curious to learn more about people who have ruined their days, their careers or their whole lives, don't ask them at a cocktail party. Successful people will sometimes talk about failures in their early careers, but usually, we don't want to admit to our mistakes. After all, who wants to buy stock in a company where the CEO confesses that he is a screw-up? Who would purchase a book from an author who writes only about their terrible life?

Failure is also a tough topic to research. There aren't any colleges that offer a degree in Failure Studies. There are tens of thousands of industry conferences in the United States every year, but the first one to focus exclusively on failure was Failcamp Philly in 2008. It didn't make it another year. Another event, FailCon 2009 in San Francisco, drew a larger crowd. Still, both events are struggling for attention. It doesn't seem like failure gets much press.

Seemingly the only ongoing discussion of the topic is the excellent online magazine *Failure* (www.failuremag.com), whose byline insists: "It's an option." Since 1999 this journal has chronicled weird and fascinating examples of unimpressive results. Their home page is not without irony, as it lists the *least* popular articles from the *Failure* archives.

Fading conferences and snarky websites aside, there are two disciplines that are obsessed with failure. The world's engineers have a precise definition of failure and are constantly studying what went wrong to prevent it in the future. The other field that loves to talk about failure is the practice of *usability*. Specialists in this area are interested in how easy it is for people to use systems, devices and visual displays. For engineers, failure is the most serious issue to be avoided. For usability experts, user failure is the best source of information for new designs.

Most of the time, well-engineered systems operate without any problems. According to the Federal Highway Administration, there are over 500,000 active bridges in the United States. Every day, millions of people drive across them without even a second thought. These structures must be properly built and managed to ensure our safety, yet we rarely consider their value. Their success is mostly unnoticed.

But on Wednesday, August 1, 2007, one bridge did not function as designed. At 6:05PM, a structure in Minneapolis, Minnesota collapsed, killing thirteen people and injuring nearly one hundred more.

While rescue workers rushed to the scene and the community reached out to those affected by the tragedy, engineering teams from the National Transportation Safety Board (NTSB) began to research the cause of the failure. After over a year of comprehensive study and analysis, the NTSB released a final report identifying four main factors that caused the failure.

First, key parts of the bridge should have been thicker and stronger. The I-35W bridge was built using *gusset plates*, a civil engineering technique that uses thick sheets of metal to connect beams and girders together. Had these plates been stronger, the bridge would not have fallen. This type of failure is a **design failure**, because it occurred as part of the bridge's construction. Had the original engineering team foreseen this issue, they could have made the gusset plates thicker and likely prevented this accident.

Second, ongoing maintenance increased the overall weight of the bridge itself. In the decades that passed after the bridge opened in 1967, crews resurfaced the structure and eventually added a total of *two inches* of additional concrete to the road surface. This increased the "dead load" of the bridge by 20%. The increase contributed to the loss of the bridge. This is called a **maintenance failure**, as the bridge was not properly managed over time.

Image courtesy of United States Coast Guard

Third, the NTSB study showed that routine efforts to check the status of the bridge were inadequate. Funding cuts meant that teams did not arrive as frequently as recommended, and photos from a 2003 review even showed the gusset plates bowing. This type of failure is an **inspection failure**, since it's an error on the part of the people responsible for confirming the health of the bridge.

Finally, it was revealed that on the day of the collapse, heavy construction vehicles and equipment were located on the bridge just above the weakest point of the structure. The board estimated that all the machinery, sand and water comprised an additional 578,000 pounds of weight for the bridge to support. These structures are designed to carry traffic, but not necessarily designed to support the incredible loads of construction crews. Therefore, this last problem is a **usage failure** on the part of that team.

Not surprisingly, the Minneapolis bridge disaster and the NTSB report ushered in a wave of changes in these areas. Hundreds of new bridges were quickly inspected, new federal funding was reserved to repair structures marked as "deficient" and policies for design, construction, inspection and maintenance were updated. **The engineering community reacted to failure the way it always does: by refining practices to prevent failure in the future.**

The view of failure held by engineers is tremendously practical for engineering. It is also incredibly effective: the Minneapolis disaster was the exception, not the rule. Most civil engineering projects are reliable and useful. **To an engineer, failure is never desired.** But if it occurs, a failure is studied in great detail to first determine causes and second, make changes to standard practices.

The usability profession takes the opposite perspective. Failure is embraced, not avoided. To usability experts failure is the best possible result of a test. The details of that failure, however, rarely make it out of the lab.

A great example of usability and failure is the story of the scrollbar. If you're near a computer, go and find an example of one of these components. You can open just about any web page, word processing document, image or anything else you like, and it will surely be there. The scrollbar is universal and is easily located no matter the brand of computer or application.

Scrollbars have become a standard user interface technique for letting the user "pan" the screen. You can click the little arrow buttons at either end of the scroll bar to move the view area. Alternately, you click-and-drag on the scrollbar knob (also called the "thumb" or "shuttle") to slide the view up or down. Dragging the knob is much faster than clicking the arrows and gives the user more control.

Decades ago, when the first graphical user interfaces were being created for computers, someone must have tested this feature of a scrollbar with an actual user. There's no way of figuring out when this first happened and probably no record of it occurring, but someone must have sat down with an early mouse in front of a black and white monitor to click and drag the scrollbar thumb up and down. You can still do this today on your own computer to see the results.

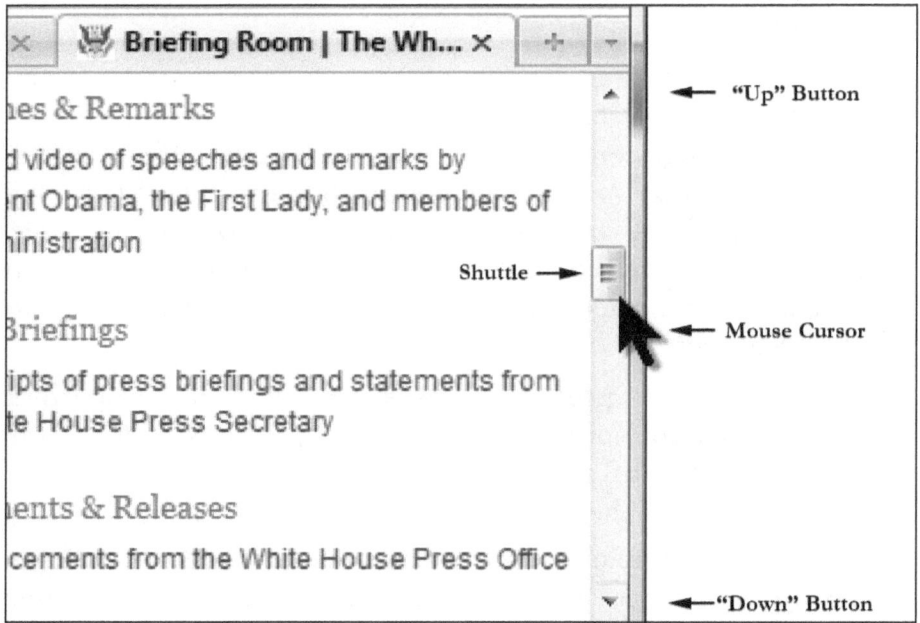

Typical scrollbar, with up/down buttons and shuttle visible

During this test, someone must have realized that it's actually pretty hard to move the mouse very quickly in a perfectly straight vertical line. Users will tend to move the cursor off of the scrollbar thumb. The mouse button is still depressed, but the cursor is no longer on top of the shuttle. Moving the mouse away cancels the operation. This frustrates the user who may then decide not to use the scrollbar in this way. The failure is evident.

However, this mythical usability test presents an easy solution. What if the scrollbar allowed the user to wander off the shuttle a little while dragging? Even a few pixels in either direction would alleviate this issue and eliminate this kind of failure from occurring in the future. And indeed, if you're sitting near a computer now with a vertical scrollbar on the screen, you can see this design in action. Click on the scrollbar thumb and drag it up and down. With your mouse button still depressed, pull the cursor a little ways *away* from the scrollbar. The dragging is still effective!

With some experimentation, you can find the exact margin of error that the scrollbar allows. Some programmer whipped up this solution years ago and it has stuck. Noticing the failure was tremendously useful. Interestingly, there doesn't seem to be any detailed analyses of scrollbar tolerances in the literature of usability and interface design. This is a failure that was identified, corrected and mostly forgotten.

Both engineering and usability value failure, but approach it from different contexts. For people who build bridges failure is to be avoided at all costs. When something goes wrong, the event must be studied extensively so the entire discipline can learn and change its ways. But for usability experts, failure is fantastic news. Had no one ever tested a scrollbar with a user, millions of people would have been annoyed (or at least made less productive) by the behavior of this interface element. Unlike engineering, in usability the reaction to failure is an immediate fix. There is generally no long analysis of design, maintenance, inspection and usage of the system. Ask any usability specialist: they love to find a problem and rapidly implement a solution.

These two disciplines provide significant insight for how we should view failure. Making mistakes means being prepared to study them in detail. Making mistakes should not be avoided; instead, mistakes must sometimes be pursued. We are so accustomed to the idea that failure is embarrassing it's hard to accept the engineering mindset of dutiful review of failure. Furthermore, we are so strongly conditioned to characterize failure as unacceptable that the usability viewpoint of failure as *desired* seems backwards. Who wants to fail on purpose and then obsess over why we failed? That seems like a double dose of bad ideas.

Yet, there is tremendous value in looking at failure in a new way. The outcome of these two perspectives can be summed up in a quote by Gordon Moore, co-founder of Intel: "With engineering, I view this year's failure as next year's opportunity to try it again. Failures are not something to be avoided. You want to have them happen as quickly as you can so you can make progress rapidly."

It's time to throw away the old adage that "Failure is not an option." No, failure *is* an option. For engineers, failure is the best way to learn. For usability experts, failure is the best place to start. In fact, failure is often the *best* option. Failure gives us a context for success.

If these two professions have learned so much from the practice of failure, why can't the rest of us do the same? Perhaps it is because so much of our attention is wrapped up in the obsession with unintended errors. The fear of failure paralyzes us. The memory of failure stings us. The chain of how our failures impact others frightens us. These negative emotions can make it hard to talk about failure, much less study and pursue it.

But for now, let's try to take on a new perspective toward failure. Let's try to recognize that failure might be something which is actually good for us. Let's try starting our next project by failing.

Chapter 2

Before Starting, Try Failing

> The knowledge gained from failures is often instrumental in achieving subsequent successes. In the simplest terms, failure is the ultimate teacher.
> – David Garvin

It might seem like the best way to start is by succeeding. After all, if your team wins the season opener, you have set the stage for a great year. But just as failure is sometimes a prelude to success, success is also a prelude to failure. If you start at the top, any new place you might go is on the way to the bottom. Winning may be the goal, but it's not always the best place to begin.

This sounds depressing, as if all success is doomed to be followed by failure. This is obviously not the case. Rather, we should acknowledge that success is often a long process. We can't always describe the tenets of our victory on the first day of our journey. What if instead of trying to emulate success we instead start by failing? What if we began in the place we're afraid we might end up? Doing so gives us the opportunity to climb higher and cover more ground. Our smartest choice may well be to learn and grow from a certain and intentional defeat.

Starting out failing is not only a curious concept; it's also the reality for many people throughout history. Consider the story of one individual from rural Ohio who was born into a working class family. As a boy, Hiram managed to convince his local congressman to recommend him to the United States Military Academy at West Point. Unfortunately, the congressman screwed up his name on the application and to avoid the bureaucratic hassle, the young man decided to just adopt the false moniker as a nickname. He eventually graduated in the bottom half of his class, and was assigned the job of a quartermaster to manage supplies and equipment.

Although the young man was married, he could not afford to support his wife and children on his military wages and thus lived alone while posted on the west coast. After ten years in the Army, Hiram had only advanced to captain. He then resigned with no notice or explanation—many believed he was caught drunk while serving duty and given the chance to leave without a formal court martial.

Hiram moved to Missouri to work a farm owned by his father-in-law but was unable to turn a profit. He brought his family to St. Louis where he began a job as a bill collector, but failed at this job as well. Finally, Hiram went to work for his own father as an assistant in a small shop in Illinois. It appeared as if the middle-aged man would spend the rest of his life in obscurity.

But in 1861, President Abraham Lincoln announced a call for volunteers following the first shots of the civil war. Hiram organized a group of recruits and quickly impressed the Governor of Illinois, who asked him to lead the training efforts for the state militia. Hiram pressed for a field command and was given authority over the 21st Illinois Infantry.

Hiram's first battle was unremarkable. Three months later, however, he captured Fort Henry and Fort Donelson from the Confederates. At the latter, Hiram's unit was ambushed while he was away from the fort. Yet the officer remained cool and organized a counterattack the following day, forcing the two senior commanders to flee. Hiram then hit a stroke of amazing luck: the remaining Confederate officer was Brigadier General Simon B. Buckner, a classmate of Hiram's from West Point. He demanded "No terms except unconditional and immediate surrender." Buckner relented and gave over control of 12,000 men. Hiram became an overnight national success. The papers used Hiram's incorrect school name of "Ulysses S." to form a famous moniker: "Unconditional Surrender" Grant.

For his efforts at Forts Henry and Donelson, President Lincoln commissioned him as a major general. He went on to earn a difficult win at Shiloh and a brilliant victory at Vicksburg. Grant continued to rise and by 1864 was appointed General-in-Chief of all the armies of the United States. He orchestrated much of the last two years of the war and ran the overland campaign. Grant also forced the final Confederate surrender by Robert E. Lee at the Appomattox Court House.

General Grant's leadership earned him international prestige and carried him to the White House as America's 18th president. He served for two terms, helped to enforce civil rights for African-Americans, appointed the first Native American to the Commission of Indian Affairs, created the office of The Surgeon General and established the Department of Justice.

Yet despite all of this success, Grant continued to face failure. After his presidency he was swindled out of his remaining savings and forced to sell his prized Civil War mementos. Desperate for money and now dying of cancer, Hiram decided to publish his life story with the hopes that the proceeds would support his family. As disease began to overtake him, he began to write more furiously, sometimes scrawling fifty pages in a single day. As he neared the end of the book and the end of his life, Grant was unable to walk. He finished his manuscript on July 18, 1885 and died five days later. This final combination of failure and success paid off. The book became wildly popular and Grant's family earned nearly half a million dollars from the proceeds.

Hiram "Ulysses" Grant's many accomplishments in life came as a result of being hardened by failure. His modest roots and long history of struggle prepared him for difficult trials. Grant's successes were preceded by many embarrassing failures. It was on the eve of what might have been the most devastating moment in his life that he was saved from total humiliation. The first day of the battle at Shiloh had been costly for the Union, and a prominent politician visited President Abraham Lincoln to call for Grant's dismissal.

The two men talked late into the evening and there were many sound arguments made to replace Grant with another general. Finally, sometime after 1AM, the President responded with a simple statement on the soldier's character and ability: "I can't spare this man. He fights."

It's not surprising that Abraham Lincoln held "Ulysses" Grant in such high regard. Lincoln, too, had lived a life marked by hardship and failure. The future president was born in 1809 in a one-room log cabin. His family, poor and struggling to pay some costly legal fees, resettled in Indiana in 1816. Lincoln's only brother, Thomas, died as an infant when Abe was three. His sister died in childbirth at age 21. When Abe was nine years old, his mother died from milk poisoning. And although Lincoln established a strong bond with his stepmother, he became more distant from his biological father over time. In fact, he considered his old man to be a failure and lent him money in later years.

After leaving home, Abraham Lincoln tried to start a family. His first true love was a woman named Ann Rutledge, but she became ill and died before they could be married. This loss plunged Lincoln into a deep depression which plagued him for the rest of his life. Had Rutledge survived, he might not have learned to overcome failure and thus achieve such legendary greatness.

Abe later met Mary Todd; however, their relationship was rocky. They were engaged to be married on January 1, 1841, but when the day came, Lincoln cancelled the wedding and ended the relationship. They saw each other at a party many months later, rekindled their love and were finally married the following year.

The couple had four children, but tragically, only one would survive to adulthood. Eddie died in 1850, just one month short of his fourth birthday. Willie passed at age 11, while Lincoln was in the White House. Thomas "Tad" Lincoln managed to survive his father, but died at 18 as well. Abe's own father passed in 1851. Virtually all of the significant people in Lincoln's life died long before any of his famous accomplishments.

At the same time, the future president's working life was also filled with troubles. His first real job in a general store lasted for only a year before the business failed. He served in the Illinois militia in a local Indian conflict but saw no action. He ran for the Indiana General Assembly in 1832 but came in eighth place out of thirteen. Then Lincoln tried to start a business, which also failed. Still unable to get a job, friends helped him to get government appointments to serve as the town postmaster and assistant to the county surveyor. He had no training for either job, but was able to scrape by on the meager salary. However, this was not enough to cover his business debt so the local sheriff seized his possessions as part of frontier bankruptcy proceedings.

Then, Lincoln's life started to turn around. He ran again for the Illinois General Assembly in 1834 and won a seat. He was reelected in 1836, 1838 and 1840. He served one term in Congress from 1847-1849. In agreement with Whig Party principles—which insisted that party members should serve only one term to make room for others—he returned to Springfield to a successful law practice. And although he was pressured out of the election for Senate in 1854 and lost the senate race of 1858, it was the latter that catapulted him to national fame. The debates against Stephen Douglas earned Lincoln widespread acclaim. Two years later, in 1860, Abraham Lincoln was elected as President of the United States. His failures paved the way for success. His life is an essential part of the story of America.

Of all of Lincoln's efforts throughout his lifetime and presidency, none had a more lasting impact than the Emancipation Proclamation. This document, along with the Thirteenth Amendment to the U.S. Constitution, changed the fate of millions of African Americans. Of all the people freed by President Lincoln, one in particular is another great example of the story of success and failure. This young man was born nearly 100 years later in Brooklyn, New York. His name is Michael Jordan.

Most would have considered the teenage Michael Jordan as unremarkable. His grades, lifestyle and activities were average. But soon after entering high school, Michael Jordan faced a difficult failure. He tried out for the varsity basketball team but didn't make the cut. The future professional athlete considered this to be the worst day of his childhood.

He later told sportswriter Bob Green, "I went to my room and I closed the door and I cried. For a while I couldn't stop. Even though there was no one else home at the time, I kept the door shut. It was important that no one hear me or see me."

Michael Jordan's devastation at this failure first manifested as grief. But soon, those feelings turned to spite. Even though he was friends with many of the players on the varsity squad, he refused to cheer for them. Jordan told biographer Sam Smith that "I guess I wanted them to lose to prove that they had made a mistake by leaving me off the team."

The loss of this opportunity nearly cost Jordan his entire future. Although he grew four inches, at 6'3" he was not even listed among the top 300 high school prospects at the start of his senior year. Most of the major college basketball programs did not know he existed. Yet, Jordan continued to train, waking himself up nearly every morning at sunrise to complete challenging drills. He was determined to transform his failures into success.

The only notable scout who paid any attention to him was Roy Williams, an assistant coach at a state school who had not won a championship in twenty years. When Williams sent his head coach to visit Jordan, the two spoke more about education than basketball. Without many choices, Jordan ended up enrolling at the University of North Carolina in the fall of 1981. The young man had no idea that this season would be the catapult that powered his future.

The story of the 1982 NCAA championship game is one of the most famous in sports history. Freshman player Michael Jordan made the final shot to beat Georgetown 63-62. Jordan's career skyrocketed. He soon joined the NBA, where his performance is unrivaled. Having played in over 1,000 games, he not only set but continues to hold the all-time record for highest points-per-game average.

By retirement, Jordan had earned the title of legend. He revolutionized virtually every aspect of the game. As fellow player Earvin "Magic" Johnson states: "There's Michael Jordan and then there is the rest of us."

Jordan himself is fond of discussing the role of success and failure in his own career:

> I've missed more than 9000 shots in my career.
> I've lost almost 300 games.
>
> Twenty-six times, I've been trusted to take
> the game winning shot and missed.
>
> I've failed over and over and over
> again in my life.
>
> And that is why I succeed.

These many victories and failures on the court have not been without challenges as well. Jordan has always struggled with the balance between personal victory and team spirit. The desire for his high school varsity team to lose stayed with him. In 1990, Jordan publicly criticized his Chicago teammates during the NBA Eastern Conference finals. Shortly thereafter, the Bulls lost their chance at the championship through a series of bad games. Many critics blamed Jordan's attitude for ruining the season.

In the meantime, Michael Jordan's affinity for gambling was becoming more and more apparent. In 1992, several checks surfaced showing in excess of $100,000 in payoffs. Jordan later revealed under oath that a sum of $57,000 he paid to an associate was not in fact a business loan but instead a gambling debt. Another million dollars in potentially illegal activities came to light as Jordan faced the court of public opinion.

The greatest personal blow to Michael Jordan's life had nothing to do with money or basketball. On July 23, 1993, James Jordan Sr. was murdered at a rest area in North Carolina. Later that year, Michael Jordan resigned from the Chicago Bulls, stating that the loss of his father helped to shape the decision.

As we all know, Jordan rose from the ashes to play again. He stunned the sports world with a brief run toward Major League Baseball, and then returned to the NBA—not once, but twice more. Since his final retirement in 2003, Michael Jordan continues to spend time on various business interests and charitable endeavors as well as helping his two sons begin their own basketball careers. Though his life story is not yet complete, we know his name will continue to shine in the annals of history. As the NBA Encyclopedia notes: "By acclamation, Michael Jordan is the greatest basketball player of all time." That success began by failing to make his high school team.

"Air Jordan" had many triumphs and tragedies, but none is quite as curious as the release of the 1996 film *Space Jam*. The movie, produced by Warner Bros., featured Michael Jordan along with a cast of animated characters such as Bugs Bunny and Daffy Duck. In some respects, the film did well: grossing $230M despite a price tag of only $8M. Noted critics like Leonard Maltin and Roger Ebert gave the film positive reviews. But at the same time, many attacked the project for its crass commercialism. Fans of Jordan called the movie "demeaning to basketball." Whatever the outcome, Michael Jordan never made another full-length movie again.

Cases like *Space Jam* demonstrate that it's not always easy to tell whether an outcome is a failure or a success. Even though the filmmakers turned a profit, many of Jordan's supporters complained bitterly. Warner Bros. may have succeeded in making money, but they failed to lure one athlete into a second career in the movies. In this case, judging the event as a win or loss doesn't depend on the scoreboard, but rather on individual points of view.

This wouldn't be the first time that Warner Bros. stumbled. They became involved in the movie business just after the turn of the century, but weren't able to sign on any major actors or any big pictures. Facing bankruptcy in 1923, the owners bet the company on an obscure script. The lead for this film was a foreign actor who was almost entirely untested. Of course, we all know that Warner Bros. survived, but what you may not know is that the star of *Where the North Begins* was a German Shepard named Rin Tin Tin! Soon after, the dog became Warner Bros.' highest grossing star. He earned the unbelievable sum of $1,000 per week.

With technology changing, Sam Warner urged the studio to invest in adding "synchronized sound." His brother Harry pushed back, famously stating, "Who the hell wants to hear actors talk?" The reticence probably contributed to continued losses for Warner Bros. When Harry finally relented, it was only for movies with background music. It appeared that Warner Bros. would continue to focus almost solely on the "pictures" in motion pictures.

Their first significant film to make use of audio tracks, *Don Juan*, was well received but did not recover its production costs. By the spring of 1927, it looked like curtains for Warner Bros. Their competitors began distributing movies with incidental music with considerable success. Because the company moved too slowly toward sound technology in movies, they were about to be made obsolete by the other major studios.

Once again, the management team at Warner Bros. decided to bet the company on one project, but this time more was at stake than a canine acting career. To help finance the film and keep the company running, Harry Warner sold $4M of his personal stock. By the time production was in full swing, Harry had stopped taking a salary, pawned the family jewelry and moved his wife and children into a small apartment. There is even some evidence that the star of film was asked to make an investment.

However, even *finding* a lead had been a challenge. Warner Bros. had signed George Jessel to the role the previous year. Once the actor found out about the money troubles at the studio, he became nervous. After a read-through of the script, Jessel blew a gasket and left. Warner Bros. scrambled to find a replacement and ended up with another financial gamble: one of the most expensive and well known actors of the time.

People weren't the only problem at Warner Bros. Sam Warner was a strong advocate of Vitaphone, a new sound technology which was far superior. However, the system was complex and precarious. Although the movie running time was only eighty-nine minutes, the projectionist had to juggle fifteen film reels and fifteen fragile audio discs, each of which had to be perfectly synchronized. One false move at the New York premiere and the company would be ruined.

Warner Bros. faced perhaps their most calamitous failure one day before opening night. Sam Warner, exhausted from his constant efforts to perfect their use of the Vitaphone technology, developed a sinus infection. His condition grew worse over the last month of post-production. Warner was then hospitalized and finally succumbed to pneumonia and a cerebral hemorrhage. His obsession with bringing even better sound to movies was a major factor in his demise.

Sam Warner died on October 5, 1927. The three surviving brothers missed the premiere as they flew home for the funeral. Still grieving, they discovered that their film *The Jazz Singer* and its star Al Jolson were a huge success, earning them more than any other movie they had ever made. The risks had paid off and Warner Bros. went down in history as the producer of the first "talkie."

The movie business is full of failures and successes. Much of the early work of Warner Bros., for example, was destroyed in a terrible fire in 1934. That year closed out with a loss of $2.5 million. Next, the company produced a major flop with *A Midsummer Night's Dream*. Jack Warner made a huge mistake the soon afterward when he refused to buy the film rights to a novel by a first-time author. That's right: Warner Bros. passed on the chance to make *Gone with the Wind*.

33

❖ ❖ ❖ ❖ ❖

There's no limit to the number of stories of famous people and organizations who started out by failing. When Bette Davis attended drama school in New York, she had a classmate who was sent home because she had "no future at all as a performer." That student was Lucille Ball. And when Bette Davis was later invited to Hollywood, the studio employee assigned to meet her at the train station left because he saw nobody who "looked like an actress." This may have been the same genius who scribbled a note reading: "Can't act. Can't sing. Skinny. Balding. Dances a little." Those were words describing an early screen test for Fred Astaire.

It's not just to movie business that is filled with screw-ups. A young man named Tim Berners-Lee attended Oxford University, but was banned from using computers there because he was "hacking." Berners-Lee later invented the World Wide Web and the first web browser. Over the course of ten years, Rowland Hussey Macy opened four dry goods stores, each of which failed. His fifth became the famous Macy's department store. Vincent Van Gogh manage to sell exactly one painting during his lifetime, battling mental illness and poverty to produce over 2,000 works of art. All of us can find inspiration in the failures of our heroes as well as in their successes. Doing it wrong is often a prerequisite for doing it right.

If the people we admire managed to turn failure around, perhaps there is something meaningful in failure itself. What if failure isn't just a sign post, but an interesting destination? What if failing has some benefit? What happens when instead of always trying to succeed, we try to fail?

We must give ourselves permission to fail. The famous people of our world have failed miserably and lived to tell about it. As Edward De Bono says: "It is better to have enough ideas for some of them to be wrong, than to be always right by having no ideas at all."

We can't always succeed by copying success. Yet the lives of people we admire have something else in common: they often *begin* with failure. Although counterintuitive (and a little bit crazy), failing *on purpose* may be the most effective way to prepare for future achievements. If we are going to become experts at success, perhaps we should also become experts in failure. We may need to take the plunge and intentionally set out to do things wrong.

Chapter 3

Great Ways to Fail Better

> Failure underscores the need to take chances. The cliché is right: If you take no risks, there will be no rewards. And if you are taking risks, almost by definition, you are going to fail at some point.
> – Jeff Wuorio

Failing on purpose. It sounds like a terrible idea, doesn't it? Who wants to fail? Yet if we want to succeed—and success *requires* failure—maybe we need to at least think about what happens if we *set out to fail*. We know that when we try to succeed, we sometimes fail anyway. Does trying to fail mean we might sometimes succeed?

The following pages list several ideas for failing better than ever before. Here's your chance to be a big success at failure.

Strategy #1: Give yourself permission to fail

If you've ever seen an improvised comedy show, you may find yourself wondering how the actors are able to come up with such amazing material without any preparation. In fact, some audience members are skeptical that "improv" is truly improvised. This suspicion is further reinforced when performers talk about going to "rehearsal." How can you practice what you plan to make up on the spot?

According to legendary improv teacher Keith Johnstone, the secret is *expecting* to fail. A popular exercise among improvisers during practice is to form a circle, and then take turns stepping into the middle to speak the words: "I've failed." The performer is encouraged to smile and take a bow, and receive uproarious applause from the rest of the group.

When the "I've failed" game is first explained, it seems completely pointless. Shouldn't performances be dynamic and filled with interesting content? The procedure sounds scripted and boring. Yet, stepping into the circle is a profound experience. Stating "I've failed" releases a hidden tension that has been long ignored. Since the game doesn't require explaining the details of the failure, the improviser does not feel any pressure to apologize or admit weakness. And best of all, the instant affirmation feels terrific. People are applauding you because you are happy that you failed, when in reality, you succeeded at playing the game.

This activity is designed to change our viewpoint about failure. Not only should failure be celebrated, the exercise seems to imply, failure should be *pursued*. Each player receives explicit authorization to proclaim their failure. If the group gives you permission to screw up, you can feel comfortable in doing so for yourself. Failure becomes interesting and enjoyable, and serves as the foundation for great theater.

If you can make it to an improv comedy show, you can witness the role of failure first-hand. The best moments on stage are when it's clear to the audience that the players aren't quite sure what to do next. They joyously stumble along and try to stay in character while the crowd laughs uncontrollably. Failure is the secret to their success.

It's easy to find historical examples where *permission to fail* was the foundation of success. Near the end of the 19th century, Thomas Edison set out to create the first commercially viable electric light bulb. Many had tried before, but their versions would burn out after only a few hours or were far too expensive. Edison knew that he would fail many times before discovering a workable solution. Had he known the depths of his failure, he might never have started the project in the first place.

In January of 1879 the team at Edison's laboratory in Menlo Park began testing possible materials to serve as the light bulb filament. The search began with various metals and minerals, but soon expanded to plant fibers. Nothing seemed to work. Edison contacted biologists and botanists in the field and asked them to send exotic samples. "Before I got through," he later recalled, "I tested no fewer than 6,000 vegetable growths, and ransacked the world for the most suitable filament material."

Edison's tenacity enthralled the public and the press. Because he had given himself permission to fail as a precursor to success, he refused to even use the word failure. "I have not failed 10,000 times," said Edison. "I have successfully found 10,000 ways that will not work."

Of course, the rest of Edison's story is well known. He did eventually find a workable solution and his name is synonymous with the electric light today. Permission to fail was the foundation of Edison's success. He knew he would get it wrong thousands of times before getting it right.

This is the same power that teachers give to students when instead they offer to ignore their lowest grade in final calculations. It's why great restaurant managers tell their servers: "You'll lose your job if you break the rules, but not if you make mistakes."

Permission to fail is why writers have editors and why children's bikes have training wheels. Give yourself permission to fail and watch what happens to you.

Strategy #2: Make a mess

We think of success as being clean and orderly. Consider the silky, flawless face of a fashion model or a gorgeously executed maneuver in competitive sports. The winners in life often seem impossibly perfect.

Yet we know that victory often requires getting dirty. When Berlin-based artist Dane Mitchell wanted to enter a prestigious modern art competition in New Zealand, he knew he would need something amazing to take the top prize. But instead of preparing a piece for exhibition and flying halfway across the world, he simply called the gallery as the other contestants were unpacking their work. Mitchell asked the staff to pick up the discarded wrapping and packing material from the other entries and place it into a single pile on the floor. That was his entry, titled "Collateral." Dane Mitchell won the Waikato National Contemporary Art Award and a cash prize worth $10,000.

Many were not pleased with this outcome. Local artist Collette Fergus called the event a "sad mockery of us all and an embarrassment to the arts community." But the episode does show that sometimes junk can be a path to success—even if you're just shuffling around in someone else's clutter by giving instructions from afar. In this contest, the most compelling art was not what was carefully prepared but instead what was casually discarded.

Sometimes making a mess leads to discovery. The first words that Alexander Graham Bell spoke into the telephone occurred right as he spilled battery acid on himself. Had he not yelled "Mr. Watson, come here!" one of Graham's competitors might have beaten him to the patent office. A little sloppiness went a long way.

At about the same time that Bell was working on the telephone, a newspaperman named Christopher Latham Sholes tried and failed to build a typesetting machine. He then found a partner who helped him build a ticket printing device, and another who hoped to transform it into something which could ink letters and words at the touch of a button. After a frustrating year with little progress, half of his partners quit and Christopher Sholes was left alone with his machine and his investor.

It was then that failure turned to desperation. Recognizing that court reporters would be target customers, Sholes and his new colleague sent expensive prototypes to noted stenographers around the country. One of these court reporters was James O. Clephane.

The reviews were not kind. According to historian George Iles, "Clephane was so unsparing in his tests that [it was] not seldom he reduced a machine to ruin." He would smash keys, break levers and rods. As quickly as Sholes could produce a new version for Clephane, the stenographer would find some fault in the design. It was as if Sholes sent expensive, custom-built machinery halfway across the country which was then sent back utterly destroyed.

Clephane did more than test each device. He was also a master wordsmith and would send a caustic letter along with the broken devices. It must have been horrifying for Sholes to build a prototype worth the equivalent of $4,000 today only to have it returned as a busted heap of parts. Each shipment included a handwritten note describing its many failings in painful and exacting detail.

Eventually, Christopher Sholes lost his temper. "I am through with Clephane!" he screamed to his financier, James Densmore. The businessman replied:

> This candid fault-finding is just what we need. We had better have it now than after we begin manufacturing. Where Clephane

points out a weak lever or rod let us make it strong. Where a spacer or an inker works stiffly, let us make it work smoothly. Then, depend upon Clephane for all the praise we deserve.

The wake of debris from the testing process made it possible for Sholes' invention to become a success. George Iles later wrote that the typewriter "had been developed under the fire of an unrelenting critic." James Densmore's words contain something profound. Credit should go not to the inventor, but the destroyer. Christopher Sholes may have designed the elegant mechanisms of first successful typewriter, but the more important genius came from the chaos of rigorous, destructive testing. Failure after maddening failure made it possible for the invention to succeed.

However, there were still challenges ahead for Christopher Sholes. The Remington Arms company purchased manufacturing rights for the typewriter and soon discovered a new problem. As the first customers became more proficient with the product, they found that the faster they typed, the more likely they were to jam the machine.

Sholes' design used a series of hammers, called *typebars*, to strike against an inked ribbon and thus mark the paper. These would fall back into place due to gravity, but because the keys had been laid out alphabetically, letters that commonly appeared together (such as "st") would often stall the machine.

To solve the problem, Christopher Sholes made another mess on purpose. He rearranged the keyboard so that letters that were most frequently typed in sequence were placed far apart from each other. Typists eventually learned to type quickly, but they had to puzzle their way through a jumbled keyboard. By the time people mastered the new layout, the jamming problem had been solved by other approaches. We still have this messy layout today. It's called QWERTY.

A strategy for failure may involve a little intentional disorganization. Instead of trying to tackle that pile of papers on your desk from the top to the bottom, try shuffling them randomly to gain a fresh perspective. Reorder your email inbox so that old messages appear at the top, or sort them by their subject. You may see new patterns or spot information which wasn't previously apparent.

If actually making a mess is too much for you, try *fantasizing* about what would happen if you made a mess. What might you find if you dumped those boxes in the back of the office? What would happen if you tried some crazy ingredients in an old standby recipe?

The worst thing that can happen when you try to fail is that you succeed at failing. This is also the best thing that can happen, because it's what you set out to do! Make a mess. Screw things up. Do it wrong in order to find a way to do it better.

Strategy #3: Ignore warnings and wisdom

This may be the most controversial advice that one could provide about failure. Usually, a warning is well-justified. Advisories should be read carefully and followed precisely. The prevailing wisdom on some topic is often based in fact. Adhering to this advice is sound reasoning, since the best way to avoid danger is by making sure you don't do anything someone else has identified as potentially hazardous.

But if you're *trying* to fail, you may want to ignore the advice of others. You might just learn something about the reason the warning exists—if there is any reason at all. Tossing aside what everyone knows isn't just a great way to fail; it can often give us a sense of purpose. As Walter Bagehot once said, "The greatest pleasure in life is doing what people say you cannot do."

Scurvy is one of the most terrible and widespread diseases in human history. The Greek philosopher Hippocrates was the first to describe the condition in detail, and since that time hundreds of epidemics have been recorded. As nations became empires and sea power began to define the course of history, the incidence of the disease skyrocketed. Many naval missions suffered a 50% fatality rate due to scurvy. In his 1497 voyage around the Cape of Good Hope, Vasco de Gama lost 100 of 160 men to disease.

For centuries, people attributed virtually all ailments to supernatural causes. Therefore, the common wisdom was that the best way to prevent scurvy was good hygiene, plenty of exercise and high morale. Sailors were warned against eating food that was rotten or had worms. Tragically, it was this advice that led to their death: scurvy is actually *caused* by a deficit in vitamin C, a substance present in many fruits and vegetables—even if they are spoiled.

The connection between diet and scurvy was discovered, announced, ignored and forgotten dozens of times. In 1535, a disease-ridden crew commanded by Jacques Cartier landed in modern-day Quebec, where the natives cured them with a tea made from white cedar pine needles. Before the end of the century, other explorers had documented citrus fruits as effective against scurvy, but most people stuck to general wisdom about the condition. A controlled experiment was accidentally performed in 1601 on a group of four ships, when just one captain served his crew lemon juice daily. Although the discoverer, Captain James Lancaster, reported his findings to the Admiralty, the suggestion was ignored in favor of the popular opinion on the topic. The same information on scurvy was rediscovered and reported again in *The Surgeon's Mate* in 1636, and once again in a comprehensive study by physician James Lind in 1747. Again, the new information was tossed aside in favor of what everyone knew.

It was not until the round-the-world voyage of Captain James Cook (1768-1771) in which not a single crew member died of scurvy that people began to take notice. Nevertheless, it still took nearly another quarter century for the British to officially adopt a policy of citrus juice as a mandatory ration for all sailors. Although lemons were often utilized for this purpose, at that time the word "lemon" and "lime" were used interchangeably. Hence, lime juice inspired the slang term "limey" for the British—which is still in use today.

Unfortunately, the story of scurvy doesn't end there. By the middle of the 19th century, advancements in naval technology meant that most journeys were too short for scurvy to develop anyway. Citrus juice was technically made a requirement on all British ships in 1867, but in reality most ocean travelers didn't actually need it because they were only on the seas for a few weeks at most. When the Admiralty switched from lemons to limes for economic reasons, there was no obvious difference in results. Unwittingly, the cure had been replaced with something that was mostly ineffective.

The disease that everyone thought had been defeated suddenly returned. An expedition in 1875 and another one 1894 were both nearly destroyed by scurvy, even though they had plenty of rations of lime juice. In fact, the only technique that seemed to have any effect in the polar regions was the consumption of fresh meat. Somehow, crews could survive for years without contracting scurvy and without any fruits or vegetables at all, so long as they were committed carnivores. This challenged the newer conventional wisdom that lime juice prevented scurvy.

In the meantime, advances elsewhere in medicine identified bacteria as the cause of many diseases. Dr. Reginald Koettlitz, the chief physician on the 1894 voyage, suggested that some meats actually *produced* scurvy if not well-preserved or at least consumed promptly. Past success with citrus juice might have helped to kill the bacteria, Koettlitz argued, but the bad meat theory was consistent with his own experience in the field.

Koettlitz joined the famous Discovery Expedition to Antarctica of 1901-1904 where he expected to amass more evidence for this way of thinking. He carefully investigated canned meats for spoilage and tossed aside any that were suspect. Koettlitz's confidence was shattered when a sledding party returned to camp with signs of scurvy. They had only been away for three weeks.

The bacteria model of scurvy made sense, it was consistent with the evidence and the remedies that followed were usually effective. The condition occurred less frequently, which gave further support to the techniques in use. In 1907, however, two researchers at the University of Oslo accidentally produced scurvy in guinea pigs. No one had ever seen the affliction in animals before. They did it by feeding them a diet of pure grain.

Those controlled experiments proved that scurvy was actually a *deficiency* disease. After all, if animals developed scurvy in controlled conditions, it couldn't be something they ate. It had to be something they *didn't* eat. Still, the world required another thirty years of politicking and analysis to conclusively identify the culprit. Vitamin C occurs in high concentrations in lemons, pine needles, and parts of animals considered a delicacy, such as the livers or kidney. Go a couple of weeks without this essential nutrient and anyone will develop scurvy.

The quirks of history combined with popular wisdom contributed to one of the most resilient and terrifying diseases of all time. Most people accepted the common viewpoint. Adhering to this way of thinking caused the deaths of over a million sailors throughout history.

There's a fancy term for this mistake: *argumentum ad populum*. That's a Latin phrase meaning "appeal to the people" and it represents the false idea that if many believe something, it must be true. In the case of scurvy, ignoring popular opinion enabled a few to survive.

Acting despite warnings to the contrary doesn't need to be on a global scale, even if it involves national destiny on the seas. A popular myth claims that Christopher Columbus was the first to seriously suggest that the world was round and that sailing west from Europe would eventually bring you to the Far East. But the truth is that most seamen believed the earth was curved. After all, if you watch a ship advancing on the horizon, the top appears first, then the mast and sails, and finally the hull.

The explorer was not the interesting failure in this story, but the financiers. King Ferdinand II and Queen Isabella I of Spain were practically broke from fighting a war with the Moors who had invaded Spain. Columbus had already been rejected *twice* by the Portuguese and generated little more than skepticism from the English. Christopher Columbus was already a failure, and several other governments had already decided that supporting his expedition would be foolish.

Furthermore, the explorer wanted rather generous terms: to receive the title "Admiral of the Seas" as well as a percentage of all profits and governorship over any lands discovered. Worse, most of Isabella's advisers recommended against the mission. They believed, correctly, that it was much farther to the Orient than Columbus had calculated.

Nevertheless, the expedition was commissioned on borrowed funds and Columbus now enjoys a place in history. A failure to follow advice and the warnings of others led to considerable success. It is curious to note, however, that Columbus may be best remembered not for his achievement but for screwing up on his mission to find a quick route to China and India. His mistake lives on in the form of a ridiculous name for Native Americans: "Indians."

One surefire way to fail is to do the opposite of what others instruct you to do. You might realize that conventional wisdom isn't always that wise after all. And you might, like Columbus, Ferdinand and Isabella, discover something entirely different than you expected.

An old Chinese proverb advises that: "The person who says it cannot be done should not interrupt the person doing it." People who are afraid to fail always follow advice. People who believe in the transformative power of failure are sometimes prepared to listen to the words of others and then try to do the opposite.

If failure is the secret to success, we must find ways to fail more effectively. This begins by **giving ourselves permission to fail.** After all, failure is going to happen and we need to be prepared to accept it when it happens. What easier way to fail than to **make a mess?** We all look at piles of junk as evidence we've screwed up, but sometimes disorder may lead to new ideas. A clean, orderly system may be what experts recommend, but if we want to be ready to fail, we must be **prepared to ignore popular wisdom.**

These three strategies form a basis for failing on purpose, but they are only the beginning. There's more to making mistakes yet to uncover. Prepare yourself to fail in new and exciting ways.

Chapter 4

Even More Ways to Fail Better

> No one who cannot rejoice in the discovery of
> his own mistakes deserves to be called a scholar.
> – Donald Foster

If success requires perseverance, repeated failure requires tenacity. A handful of strategies aren't enough; we need more ways to fail. Like the improvisers at a late night comedy show, we not only need to give ourselves permission to fail, we need to be endlessly creative in coming up with crazy ideas for making mistakes. Here are four more ways to fail better.

Strategy #4: Avoid Recommended Tools

Often, we begin an activity by using whatever system or approach seems most applicable. When you want to attach two boards together with a nail, you use a hammer. This is probably the right piece of equipment for the job—using a rock or the heel of your shoe won't be as effective. However, using recommended tools can sometimes lead you astray. As the expression says: "If all you have is a hammer, *everything* looks like a nail."

Sometimes, the common approach has been replaced by something more advanced and more efficient. Upon entering a library, you might head for the card catalog out of habit. Using a computer terminal to find a book will probably save you time. Neither of these approaches, however, are quite as effective as placing a call to the reference desk from the comfort of your home. You're more likely to get accurate information from a librarian than an automated system, and the helpful voice on the other end of the line may even pull the book off the shelf for you to later retrieve!

Purpose-built tools are essential to many modern professions. Advanced technology is essential for people like biomedical engineer Michelle Klein, who came to the brand-new Merced campus at the University of California in 2006. Her specialty there was a field called *microfluidics*—tiny liquid-filled channels used for diagnostic testing. But when Klein arrived, the lab did not have the specialized equipment for making samples that she had used before. With a price tag of $100,000, the necessary machinery wasn't likely to come any time soon.

"I'm a very impatient person," Klein told a reporter with *Technology Review*. In her haste to begin working, she remembered a toy from her childhood—Shrinky Dinks—which could be colored with ink and the activated by heat in a standard kitchen stove. So,

Klein put together a microfluidic channel on the computer, printed it out on Shrinky Dink material and baked it in a toaster oven. The ink particles formed tiny ridges as they shrank, creating a makeshift replacement.

Klein didn't think much of her hack and assumed that once the fancy equipment arrived, her Shrinky Dink days would be over. Yet when she published a paper about her efforts, researchers from all over the world began to reach out to her. Since then, Klein has been promoted and continues to do more research with the same inexpensive children's toy.

When Michelle Klein decided to try Shrinky Dinks as a substitute method for her experiments, she likely expected to fail. Maybe using the material would provide some insight, but mostly it was a way to pass the time until the purpose-built machinery arrived. For Cory, a warehouse floor manager at a small business-to-business reseller, the situation was reversed. The recommended tools were working fine. Rather, it was the new hires that seemed to be the problem.

Cory and the other old-timers already knew all of the patterns in the operation. They had memorized the location of every part on the shelves, knew how to use the shipping labels and could easily put a complex order on a cart just from memory. However, the new employees were facing over 20,000 square feet of unfamiliar warehouse and procedures that were foreign to them. So, Cory decided to do the opposite of what was expected. Instead of spending weeks training and drilling the recent hires, he built a simple documentation system to help reduce errors and guide the new workers.

Although Cory planned to abandon the reports after a month or two, he noticed something which surprised him. The paper forms actually *increased* productivity among *all* his workers. Those who used them were able to process orders more quickly with fewer errors. Soon everyone was using the new documents and was able to finish more work in less time. Not surprisingly, Cory and his fellow employees decided to make the temporary system permanent.

We often try to ensure our success by using the tools that everyone recommends. Amateur cyclists will purchase expensive bikes used by professionals hoping they will give them an edge. High school students apply to top colleges believing these programs will guarantee success later in life. Budding writers will buy brand name Moleskine notebooks because similar pads were used by Oscar Wilde and Ernest Hemmingway. Emulating the successful is one way we try to succeed.

But if our goal is to fail, we can't always use the tools and techniques that everyone recommends. If we are going to screw up, we need to be ready to try radically different approaches to problems. We need to be prepared to accept that these choices may contribute to significant missteps. If recommended tools might lead to success, avoiding them might lead to failure. If we can fail gracefully using wildly inventive means, we have better equipped ourselves for an uncertain future.

Strategy #5: Operate out of order

If the directions have multiple instructions in a sequence, you can be sure that "Step 1" is intended to go before "Step 2." Following a path in order is supposed to lead you to success. Therefore, operating in the wrong order should lead you to failure. Taking a shortcut in unfamiliar territory will probably leave you lost and covered with poison ivy. Therefore, skipping some of the steps, following the last instructions first and tossing out the guidebook altogether is another phenomenal way to make mistakes.

The obvious advantage to operating out of order is that you may sometimes find required tasks which are actually not necessary. For example, a standard regimen at the gym is to complete your cardio first followed by a weight routine. This way, one workout session can include both endurance training and strength training.

However, starting out on the treadmill means you'll need to warm up your muscles to avoid strain. So if you reverse your workout—weights *before* cardio—you can avoid having to spend time in the cardio warm-up phase. This makes your exercise routine more efficient.

Sometimes operating out of order just means doing the unexpected. The pattern of play in the card game Hearts requires that each player *avoids* winning a hand which includes any hearts. For each heart a team collects, they gain one point. But the card game Hearts is like the game of golf: whoever manages to keep their score the lowest is the winner.

However, as any skilled player knows, the other way to win Hearts is to try the opposite strategy. This is called "shooting the moon" and is done by *intentionally* collecting all the hearts as well as the queen of spades. The rules of Hearts explain that if a team succeeds in picking up every single heart as well as the 13-point queen they are not punished with the expected twenty six points. Instead, the *other* players receive these points as a penalty. You can't always win a hand by shooting the moon, but if you do you'll earn the biggest score possible.

Skipping steps, changing the order and doing the opposite of what others expect is an effective technique in many card games. However, there's probably no game where the strategy is more powerful than in high-stakes poker.

According to the rules of the game, players aren't supposed to reveal the contents of their hands until the "call." But great poker players twist this rule using a wide variety of psychological techniques to try and modify the nature of play to their own advantage. "Advertising," for example, is a poker term that involves making obvious plays to try and communicate your style of play. If you seem to always play aggressively or conservatively, you might be able to trick other players later in the tournament. Another bit of poker lingo is the term "coffee housing" (also known as "speech play.") This is when you deliberately try to mislead other players about what is in your current hand to affect the outcome of the game.

Operating out of order is an example of failure because we are expected to follow the instructions. One example of a procedure with well-known steps is giving birth. We all know how the experience is supposed to proceed: the expectant mother waits until she believes she is having the baby, and then is rushed to the hospital at breakneck speed to endure the pains of labor.

But with modern technology, some women are turning the process on its head. They head for the hospital early at a leisurely pace, check in with the front desk and settle into their room. Once everyone is ready, they request an injection of oxytocin, a natural hormone that helps to induce labor. The entire experience occurs in the safety of the hospital without a stressful highway drive.

The practice of using drugs to jumpstart the birthing process is highly controversial. Changing the rules of the game or the order of the steps will sometimes upset other people. We must decide if the sequence cannot be changed or if we can gain a benefit by reordering them in our own way. This was the question that occurred to a new sales representative at an outbound call center.

"Every business practice has a procedure." That's what Chris heard on the first day of his new job in sales. "First, you check the spreadsheet for the next number to call. Then, you dial the number. Then, you wait for someone to pick up the call. Finally, you read the script."

Chris soon realized that because of the frequency with which he encountered voicemail and hang-ups, he was spending much of his time each day placing the receiver on the hook, dialing numbers, and waiting to be connected. So instead, Chris changed the spreadsheet from sorting by last name to sort by phone number. This meant he would be connecting to the same business for dozens of calls in a row. So before the person answering could hang up on *him*, Chris would hit zero to jump back to the operator. Then, he'd asked to be connected to the next name on his list. Skipping steps and changing the sequence might have been against policy, but it earned him more sales.

Completing tasks out of order is an easy way to fail. If you decide to drive to work first and then get dressed once you arrive, you're likely to face problems! Yet we can forget the step of driving to the store by using catalogs, online shopping, or renting movies by mail. We sometimes *do* want to "shoot first, and ask questions later." If order means success, disorder might mean failure and opportunity.

Modifying the arrangement of tasks isn't always beneficial, but it often leads to interesting failures. Doing so may also highlight that some steps are unnecessary, others could be combined, or that the process isn't optimal after all. Sometimes, the sequence in which we complete a task is just a tradition. To find out whether the steps can be changed, we must be ready for our attempts to crash and burn.

Strategy #6: Don't follow the norm

A typical pattern for success is to copy other successful people. People who have achieved weight loss tend to get plenty of exercise and eat right, so it makes sense to do the same. However, just because you may want to duplicate some of the results of others, doesn't mean you need to follow the same pattern they use. Following the norm may lead to success, so being weird on purpose can help us to fail.

The weight loss business has been around for centuries. A Presbyterian minister named Sylvester Graham (1794-1851) was among the first to develop a comprehensive diet and exercise program designed to improve physical, mental and spiritual health. Although many of Graham's recommendations were sound, many people thought he was completely crazy. He advocated vegetarianism, urged his followers not to drink alcohol and opposed additive-rich white bread. In short, Sylvester Graham was America's first health nut.

In 1837, Graham faced challenges finding places to speak in Boston under threat of riot from butchers and commercial bakers. His efforts inspired a new generation of lifestyle advocates which included Horace Greeley and John Harvey Kellogg. Graham is best remembered today for graham crackers. Ironically, the modern snack is loaded with sugar and refined flour, which Sylvester Graham despised!

Part of the reason that Graham was so successful at promoting healthy lifestyles was because his message and his system were totally bizarre. Anyone who has ever tried to lose weight knows that weird diets and unusual workout plans are strangely attractive. Perhaps doing *everything* different will yield more success than small changes.

Of course, we all know *how* to lose weight: eat better and get more exercise. Yet, some more recent examples of health campaigns are more like Sylvester Graham's rather than Jenny Craig's. Consider the emergence of "boot camps." These are early morning programs which sometimes employ screaming drill sergeants and gut-wrenching workouts. Perhaps the reason people sign up for such torture is they feel they need something extreme to succeed.

Maybe that's why a man named Steve Vaught decided that walking from Oceanside, California to the George Washington Bridge in New York City would be the right way to face his depression and shed weight off his 400-pound frame. By most accounts, Vaught failed to make much of a difference in his waistline, but he earned considerable media attention and had a life-changing experience. Perhaps it was a failure to follow the norm which drove Vaught and inspired the hundreds of thousands who checked out his website.

A similar argument can be made for the worldwide television phenomenon *The Biggest Loser*. As of 2009, a version of this show airs in the US, the UK, Australia, New Zealand, India, Israel, Brazil, Germany, Hungary and Slovakia, as well as editions for Asian and Arab markets. In the program, contestants are challenged to lose the greatest percentage of their own body weight. Even the show's title is a spin on failure. All of the players are, in some respects, people who have failed to take care of themselves. The "biggest loser" is in fact the "biggest winner."

Anyone trying to get control of their weight is familiar with failure. Most dieters yo-yo up and down on the way to their goal, if they ever reach it. Each pound lost may seem like a success until that pound is gained back again. Weight loss will contain some failure, so why not embrace that failure by going against the normal diets and exercise programs and trying something else? By embracing unusual ideas as a new way of failing, we can learn to accept failure with grace and success, and most importantly, with greater perspective.

Going through life with excess weight is even tougher if you are also short. The Spanish painter Pablo Picasso was 5'3" tall and some sources put him at 220 pounds. But as we all know, Picasso did not differentiate himself through an unusual diet or exercise program. Instead, he co-invented Cubism and revolutionized modern art.

If you look at Picasso's early work, however, you probably won't be that impressed. He was classically trained as a painter and most of his early works are copies of the styles of Renaissance masters. They were well-executed, but completely normal. When Picasso went to the Royal Academy of San Fernando at age 16, many expected him to refine his skills under their tutelage.

Picasso did not pursue the usual path. He grew bored with school and dropped out. He struggled for many years with almost no money, surviving cold winters and the suicide of a close friend. The famous painter we know today then emerged, who created harrowing paintings during his "blue period" as well as striking abstract pieces. Pablo Picasso started out following the norm and then broke away. He failed at art school and failed to find stable employment, but eventually found success by doing what no one expected.

Your own quest to fail on purpose can be inspired by these visionaries. Try breaking the rules and going against the grain. Ignore the dress code, order an unpopular dish at a restaurant or climb stairs backwards. Doing anything the way it isn't normally done gives you the opportunity to embrace it from a fresh perspective. If you set out to fail by being weird on purpose, you'll often find out and learn more about who you truly want to become.

Strategy #7: Tell white lies

We all know that you're supposed to always tell the truth. But none of us tell the truth all of the time. Sometimes we tell an outright lie saying, "No officer, I didn't know I was going so fast"—even though we knew we were speeding. Sometimes we lie by omission, saying "we just had our mechanic check this vehicle, so I can assure you that it has been thoroughly inspected"—failing to mention the problems that were found during the analysis. These are lies, and lying is wrong.

A lie is a form of failure. When we lie we fail to tell the truth. It's hard to imagine a situation in which lying on purpose in order to fail on purpose could be helpful, but consider the case of a minor deception. A "white lie" is a prevarication which helps the person speaking but would not be significant if discovered. White lies are still wrong, but they sometimes feel justified. After all, if you can get away with a lie and not suffer too much even if you are discovered, what's the harm?

The reason that these statements seem to fall in a grey area is because they are subject to interpretation. If you say you've been "working on a project," does *thinking* about the activity count? If you put an envelope in your mailbox on Sunday morning, can you claim the "check is in the mail" even though it won't even be picked up for at least twenty four hours? In both of these cases, the person telling the lie does so with good intentions. We seem to evaluate our own deceptions based on rationalizations more than definitions.

Many companies participate in white lies by making use of outsourcing. An answering service uses language that implies their staff is actually inside your own building. A post office box establishes a presence in a city without the cost of office space. An advertisement for the "best pizza in town" hints at the existence of a comprehensive study, but really just expresses a biased opinion. Are these lies or just great marketing? Perhaps a key component of any successful business is striking a balance between painfully accurate truth and potentially questionable falsehoods.

These aren't just the techniques of large organizations. White lies are part of the practice of one local business coach. She continues to publish a calendar of her training courses, even though no one has ever registered. This allows her to appear more established and successful to potential clients while she builds her business. As the French writer François de La Rochefoucauld notes, "To establish oneself in the world, one does all one can to seem established there." In more practical terms: "Fake it 'till you make it."

Perhaps it's cynical to suggest that all companies stretch the truth, but surely we should aim to be more moral as individuals. Yet many of these examples probably have you scratching your head. Should you really let your current boss know you are looking for a new job? Do you have to report that ten dollar bill you found in the park on your income taxes? Are you obligated to compliment the food at a party even if it's terrible? These situations seem so minor and commonplace to be barely worth mentioning.

We may be most concerned with downsides to these kinds of deceptions. The primary danger of telling white lies is that they may blossom into more serious falsehoods. If we attempt to maintain every fabrication, they build on each other like a house of cards. Even with this risk, however, there are some examples of actions which are technically not truthful but nevertheless very helpful. A white lie can be tremendously useful.

A simple case is the use of the "delay delivery" feature of many email programs. This utility allows you to set a time and date when a completed message will be sent to its recipients. If your boss or a client asks for a project update on Monday but you want to finish the work early, you can use this feature to make sure the email does not get sent until the weekend is over.

You are probably thinking: why lie about when you actually complete a task? Responding too quickly can set unreasonable expectations. The person receiving the message may decide (perhaps unconsciously) that you are happy to work on weekends or are ready for additional assignments. The white lie of delaying delivery can help guide others on how to treat you in the future.

Lying usually includes deceiving others, but you can also lie just in case the false claim might be helpful. Suppose you are cutting it close for an appointment and expect to show up exactly on time. Consider calling ahead to announce you might be late by a full fifteen minutes. If you beat your fake estimate, you can choose to spend a few minutes composing yourself before you go to the meeting. Or, you can arrive earlier than you announced, which shows that you are conservative *and* thoughtful.

Either way, saying you're running late when you really aren't is not just lying; it's also *giving yourself permission to fail* (Strategy #1). In addition, however, this lie gives you the chance to catch your breath and the opportunity to better present yourself to the person you are meeting. You can use the same strategy, for example, when answering the telephone.

Whenever a phone rings, the person calling is effectively telling you: *No matter what you're doing, I think you should quit that now and talk to me.* Of course, you may well want to have that conversation, but almost everyone knows that sometimes we often prefer to screen a call and return it later. When your outgoing message says "I'm not here right now," it's technically lying on your behalf.

You don't have to use an answering machine to lie with the telephone, however. A great technique is to pick up the phone and immediately answer: "I'm in the middle of something, can I call you back in five minutes?" This may well be a lie, but it gives you the chance to prepare for the call. You can review your notes, decide what you want to achieve during the conversation, or actually finish what you were working on when the phone rang.

Of course, returning a call after five minutes provides the opportunity for an even more useful lie: "Thanks for letting me call you back—I unfortunately have a commitment so I can only talk for a short while." Using this sequence of lies, you can control how you use the telephone without seeming disrespectful.

The subject of lying should include a reminder about the difference between a white lie and a noble lie. The former is an insignificant deception. If someone discovers that you set your email program to report you were "out of the office" for an extra day on either side of your vacation, you are not likely to get into any trouble.

But a "noble lie" is one that is told to protect people from a truth that would be devastating if revealed. The statement "I'm not aware of any layoff plans" is a lie designed to hide a painful reality. Failing through white lies can be an effective method for discovering smarter ways to work. Failing through noble lies is much more dangerous, because it implies a sense of superiority between parties. If one person believes another can't handle the truth, the tension can escalate into resentment and hatred.

Among the list of techniques for failing on purpose, lying is a certain technique for success. We are *never* supposed to tell lies, and yet, we do it all the time. Lies are failures, but sometimes they help. Sometimes, stretching the truth lets us reach loftier goals.

If failure is the secret to success, we must find ways to fail more effectively. We can start with **giving ourselves permission to fail**, by **making a mess on purpose** and by **ignoring wisdom and warnings**. Such techniques will help us avoid succeeding.

Yet this is only the beginning of fantastic ways to ruin everything. If there are specific tools or techniques that we are supposed to employ, we can try **discarding recommended approaches.** And if we must follow this advice, we can at least attempt to fail by **completing tasks out of order**—or in general, intentionally **fail to follow the norm**. These suggestions seem to echo Laurel Thatcher Ulrich's observation that "Well-behaved women seldom make history."

Finally, there's may be no better way to subvert social expectations than by **telling lies**. In one sense, this is the most fundamental of all failures. After all, there is no way to fail which is more pure than by providing information which is untrue, even if the distinction is subtle. A lie attempts to alter reality.

Case in point: the reference above to Ulrich's quotation about "well-behaved women" might seem like an appropriate suggestion about the historical importance of intentional misconduct. In fact, the selection of this passage is an example of a white lie and is an intentional failure. The original scholarly article where these words first appeared was about Puritan funeral sermons. In context, the remark merely notes that women in that culture held a high regard for being modest, unassuming and mostly invisible. Laurel Thatcher Ulrich wanted to comment that historians don't know much about women in Puritan society because those individuals preferred to go unnoticed.

Of course, the quotation that "well-behaved women rarely make history" has been widely misappropriated. Attaching Ulrich's name to these words without explaining the original source is a form of deception. The quote is utilized by many not because it's a fair representation of her views, but just because it's a powerful phrase. Lying may be failing, but failure is the secret to success.

The reasoning behind failing on purpose is not to glorify stupidity. Instead, this is a unique approach that helps us to accept and value failure when partaking in the process of discovering success. If we are prepared to pursue mistakes and even make attempts which we are certain will not bear fruit, we can build the humility needed to learn and grow. We can prove to ourselves that we are willing to try anything in pursuit of our goals, even something contrary to common sense.

Set out and try to fail in any way possible. If you can do it wrong, you'll have a better chance of knowing when you are doing right. It's time to win big at losing.

Chapter 5

A Methodology for Failure

> Failure is simply the opportunity to begin again,
> this time more intelligently. – Henry Ford

Le Bernadin is among the finest restaurants on the planet. They have the record for longest running four-star ranking from the *New York Times*, starting three months after they opened. The place is only one of five establishments in New York with the highest possible Michelin ranking of three stars. In 2009, *Restaurant* magazine ranked them as 15th best eatery in the *entire world*. Given all these accolades, you might be surprised to find out about one of their secret ingredients. Le Bernadin uses cheap, artificially flavored fake Swiss cheese.

For a restaurant that only accepts reservations once a month and can easily cost over $100 per person, it's shocking to discover a heavily processed product at the heart of their cuisine. But as executive chef Eric Ripert told *Newsweek* magazine, the product is not used in the food but as a benchmark to standardize the taste of sauce. "In terms of flavor, that cheese tastes identical all year long...so it gives us a reference, and we can judge fairly."

The backstory at Le Bernadin is that sometimes, the sous chefs could not accurately detect signature flavors. Perhaps the scents or tastes from other parts of the restaurant fouled up their senses. Bringing artificial Swiss into a kitchen of this caliber would usually be a colossal failure, but in this case, doing so forms the basis of a quality control methodology for success.

We recognize that failure is essential. We know that many notable people have failed throughout their lives, and we even have a series of approaches for failing on purpose. But up to this point, failure is still something which is difficult to guide with any precision. If we're going to fail, we need to be a little scientific about it!

Effective practices, whether intended to consistently succeed or consistently fail, benefit from careful contemplation. A useful concept for developing methodologies is *metawork*. The word *meta* is Greek and roughly means "about." Instead of just working, *metawork* is a focus on the *process* of work. The term is meant to encourage us to think *about* work: how we are conducting a task, why that task has value, and what steps, resources or assumptions are inherent in the way we perform the task.

You might not consider motorsports as a career where thinking about work is especially important. Yet IndyCar driver Danica Patrick was keenly focused on her driving technique when she was quoted after her first major crash:

You're driving your car and you feel frightened a little bit. We bump up against that feeling as much as we can to try and push that limit further and get comfortable there. And then push it again. So you're constantly on the brink of crashing because that's the fastest.

This is serious contemplation. Winning in the racing world requires constantly identifying, facing and overcoming fears. A team has to test the boundaries and be prepared to fail, which sometimes culminates in the terrifying experience of a crash. The secret here is not just accepting difficulties but finding ways to work through them. No matter how small the detail, a disciplined perspective on metawork suggests that we should always be thinking *about* work and how to make improvements.

When our goal is to improve efficiency at work, the temptation is always to find more effective tools. There will always be stronger raw materials and more reliable equipment with fancier features. Yet often, it seems like advanced technology *creates* as many problems as it solves.

A researcher named Erik Brynjolfsson offers a term for this phenomenon: the *productivity paradox*. This is the apparent contradiction between the tremendous increases in technology and the relatively slow increases in productivity in the larger economy. Simply put: if computers are twice as fast each year as they were the year before, why does it still take so long to get anything done?

Of course, the productivity paradox doesn't just apply to computers. The modern workplace is full of ideas designed to make us more effective but seemingly do just the opposite. Before there was voicemail, a receptionist would take your calls so that you could concentrate. Before typing was a fundamental skill, you would record memos into a Dictaphone and secretaries would transcribe your ideas. Now, we are expected to complete these tasks ourselves.

Nor does the productivity paradox have anything to do with modern technology. Long before the days of telecommuting, employees worked in sterile offices with precise hours because managers assumed they needed to personally oversee their work. Yet just as a "watched pot never boils," studies now show that many individuals are *more productive* when their boss isn't constantly hovering in the room. Furthermore, companies absorb overhead costs by providing a workspace. Sometimes it may make more sense to send the work to the worker rather than the other way around.

Perhaps the most striking example of a productivity paradox is the sad story of the cubicle. When designer Robert Probst first introduced the Action Office line in 1968, the thought was that open spaces with modular designs would provide more flexibility and increase worker output. But instead, cubicles were seen as space-efficient ways to pack more people into high-rent offices. Worse, they are usually installed in a demoralizing repetitive grid. Multiple studies have shown that cubicle workers are less productive than people in private offices or those that work from home. Just before Probst died in 2000, he apologized for his invention by calling it "monolithic insanity."

The productivity paradox shows that failure is not only rampant, but often the *direct result* of trying to make improvements. Sometimes when we attempt to design tools that will make us more effective and efficient we end up doing the opposite.

Differences in productivity are especially apparent between different individuals in different situations. Margo Beylen, a manager at Honda, experienced a dramatic variation in expectations and results first-hand. She noted, "I was asked to do more in my first week at Honda than I had done in four years at my previous job."

It might seem hard to spot the failure in this statement. Is Honda at fault for asking too much or is Beylen's former employer a company which is about to go under due to lack of assigning sufficient tasks? Neither of these guesses are a useful interpretation of the quote. Instead, we should look at the *transition* from one environment to another and the cycle of failures and successes in each.

Work, as Margo Beylen undoubtedly discovered, is not just about how much we succeed. It's also about how earnestly we fail and how effectively we learn from our mistakes. The productivity paradox here is enormous: systems designed to measure only achievement often *limit* achievement, because they make failure unacceptable. If screwing up is not an option, there is no path for dramatic innovation.

Usually, we assume that everyone either has the ability to complete a task or does not. We have fancy terms for these two concepts: competence and incompetence. Before a student begins in a foreign language course, they are *incompetent* in that language. If they complete the curriculum successfully, we say they are *competent*.

This characterization is very rough. In reality, all of us progress through a long sequence of stages between incompetence and competence. We might start out completely ignorant, but over time we gain knowledge, increase our confidence, become somewhat proficient and finally reach fluency. The path to competence has many milestones, whether we are studying calculus or becoming a master woodworker. Each level of success provides more confidence as well as more opportunities.

However, the way from failure to success is *never* a straight line. An organized methodology to follow this path must acknowledge that before we become truly competent, we reach a point of finding some success despite our limitations. During this period our sense of satisfaction is *counter* to actual results, so the state can be called *countercompetence*.

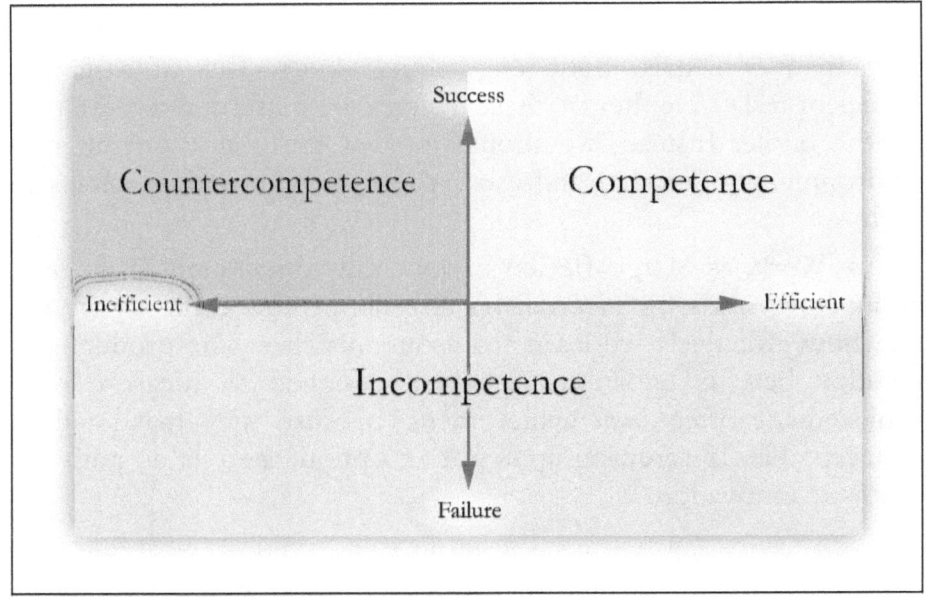

Alternate model of success and failure which includes countercompetence

There's tremendous value in including countercompetence in our understanding of how we build skills and knowledge. For one, doing so allows us to recognize that many failures are actually successes. If you're able to cook a meal poorly, you still get to eat and will have a better appreciation when you do eventually perform a miracle in the kitchen. Knowing that our initial success will be of poor quality and will take longer helps us to put the entire learning process into perspective.

Beyond acknowledging the struggle of change, recognizing countercompetence also helps to reinforce the role of specialization. We often find ourselves busy with tasks that we don't do often enough to have any real skill. Unless you spend your day changing oil, it's probably smarter to take your car to a repair shop. They will be more thorough and finish in less time. When it comes to changing oil, a professional garage is truly competent while you are likely countercompetent. Sure, you *could* get the job done; it just may take more time and probably not be done as well.

Countercompetence forms a basic methodology for failure. Consider the story of Mark, a student finishing his college career. In the final semester in the esteemed business school at a major university, Mark was required to complete an internship with a local company. He had spent four years studying sales and marketing and was excited to pursue a true corporate opportunity. But the first day on the job, he made what he later called "the biggest mistake of his career." Mark offered to try and fix a malfunctioning computer.

Like any young man, Mark saw this job as a chance to both learn more about business and advance his own career. "I was always taught that when there is work to be done, you roll up your sleeves and help out. And although sales and marketing is my passion, computers had always been a small side hobby. I figured there might be a chance I could get the machine working again."

Mark did not study information systems or computer science in school, so it took him a while to complete the task. But thanks to this success, he soon became known as the best resource in the office for technical problems. Although he had hoped to spend his time making sales calls, developing a network of resources, and honing his practical business experience, Mark received a crash course on computer system repair with no mentor, no formal training, and only a minor interest in his work. He was able to solve most problems, eventually. However, it usually took him longer than a qualified professional, and Mark knew enough about information technology to realize he was probably taking actions a true expert would consider inadvisable.

Before Mark had arrived for the internship, no one in the office had much competence troubleshooting computer problems. If a machine began to malfunction, someone would spend hours on the phone with faraway technical support personnel or lose days of work as they sent their computer out to be serviced. To the other employees, Mark seemed like a wizard, since he could achieve something they could not. "Stuff that was easy for me was amazing to them, but I really did not feel like an IT expert. I was almost afraid to answer questions, not only for fear of being wrong, but for fear of being asked more in the future."

When Mark graduated from college, he was offered a full-time position with the assurances that he would be able to focus on sales and business development. But within weeks, people started asking him to resolve network problems, un-jam printers, configure software and conduct internal technical support. He *appeared* supremely competent at fixing computers, and people began to assume that Mark was a great resource for practically any job that nobody else wanted or knew how to tackle. The company president saw Mark's apparent confidence with technology as proof he was a quick learner, and sent him out to random conferences to research new business ideas. Mark also found himself effectively in charge of an office relocation, which again reduced his focus on sales and marketing and required him to coordinate with movers, work with service vendors and manage other logistical details.

When the company started to decline, Mark only became busier. With one foot in the "profit center" of sales and the other in the "cost center" of support, he ended up working harder and harder to help keep the company afloat. Every time employees would leave, Mark would be called in to clean up after them, try to sell or re-purpose their old computers, and help the organization determine what job functions needed to be reassigned. When the company finally started to fold, Mark was one of the last people to be let go. His final task was calling second-hand resellers to try and sell company furniture.

"It was my first real job, and I learned a great deal," Mark says of his old employer. "But mostly I learned what I do not want to do in the future. For now, I want to find an opportunity at a larger company where I can have a specialized role. No more small businesses for me."

Mark's big break was a three year experience in countercompetence. Because we live in a business culture in which one would almost never say "that's not my job," Mark stumbled into a role on his first day and never really had the chance to pursue his passion or his area of training. Four years of top quality business education in sales and marketing were mostly wasted in Mark's three years as the erstwhile system administrator, research assistant and internal project manager. If only he had declined that original suggestion, Mark might have had a completely different and tremendously more positive experience with this employer.

Recognizing counter competence as an employee is usually not hard. Within weeks of starting his internship, Mark knew that the company should probably be calling a certified expert to fix computers. However, it is nearly impossible to refuse an assignment, especially if you are bright, young and eager. In fact, this belief is so ingrained with business professionals, that Mark has changed his career goals to work for a large company so as to ensure specialization and reduce the chance he will be asked to do anything outside his area of expertise.

The road from failure to success has many twists and turns. A good system for driving this highway—a *methodology*—must not only help illuminate the path but explain how to benefit from dead ends and wrong turns. We need to know our limitations and how to learn from our mistakes.

This particular area of failure has been studied extensively by two researchers at Cornell University. Everybody makes poor judgments once in a while, but Justin Kruger and David Dunning want to understand *how* we think about our own expertise. Do we understand the depths of our failure and know what to do to improve?

According to the Dunning-Kruger effect, the usual answer is no. A series of experiments demonstrate that in a variety of fields, we tend to overestimate our abilities and the quality of our thinking. In their landmark 1999 paper, the scientists explain their finding in cold academic language: "People reach erroneous conclusions and make unfortunate choices but their incompetence robs them of the metacognitive ability to realize it."

Let's take a moment to break down that statement. Anybody is capable of screwing up, but if you do so in a field where you are not an expert, you're not likely to even know that you're wrong!

You've probably experienced this in your own life, either as an expert or a novice. Perhaps you *thought* you knew what you were doing when you were filing your taxes, but a strongly worded letter later showed that you had no idea you made a mistake. Or, you may have encountered someone who speaks with confidence about an issue or field, but you secretly know they are completely clueless.

The Dunning-Kruger effect not only points out that incompetent people tend to overrate their expertise but also proves that true experts tend to dismiss their own abilities. This makes sense: highly qualified individuals are more likely to know just how much they *don't* know. They probably know people in their field who are far more respected and have a greater sense of the complexity of their universe. As physicist Niels Bohr once wrote, "An expert is a person who has made all the mistakes that can be made in a very narrow field."

There's one more crucial outcome of the Dunning-Kruger effect: novices tend to fail to recognize genuine expertise. This is because in part, we are more impressed by certainty than by details. Experts tend to know about all of the special cases and exceptions to the rules and want to make sure to include these caveats. People who are incompetent (but think they know more than they actually do) tend to make precise, unequivocal statements. Hence, real expertise is often dismissed.

Knowing about the Dunning-Kruger effect is a great way to guard against failure. You can be fairly certain that you *don't* know as much as you think you do. But awareness of this phenomenon can also be a way to pursue failure consciously. You can acknowledge that you are likely overconfident as a novice and too self-critical as an expert. And best of all, knowledge of the Dunning-Kruger effect will help to increase your faith in others. Seeking help and placing trust in those who have gone before is a crucial component of success.

There is a reason that *failure* is essential to work and that *methodology* is essential to failure. This is because so many of us are not laborers, but "knowledge workers." When famous management consultant Peter Drucker first coined this term in the late 1950s, he was referring to employees whose primary business value is their ability to gather, interpret and utilize information in a specific field.

The life of a knowledge worker is completely different from those who labored in the industrial era. A century ago, almost all jobs were entirely based on physical motion. In those positions, employees had no room for failure. Every step in the assembly of manufactured goods had to be done quickly, precisely and identically. Failure would only slow overall production, not lead to new ideas or new approaches to work.

Nowadays, it seems like almost everyone is a knowledge worker. This classification includes teachers, scientists, lawyers, nurses, engineers, social workers, photographers, journalists, technicians and clergy. And while there are still factory jobs, the world is starting to look at the intellectual capacity of these workers as much as their ability to complete menial tasks.

In fact, the entire history of management consulting can be described as the steady realization that the psychology of workers is more impactful than the measurement of work. That's not to say that everyone is a knowledge worker, but that we all have some knowledge of the work we are doing. Our perspectives on our own labor and our relationship to our environment have a tremendous influence on overall productivity. A methodical company must recognize—and analyze—the psychology of workers.

In the early 1920s, executives at the Western Electric company theorized that they might be able increase worker productivity by changing the ambient light on the factory floor. Perhaps they reasoned that a bright room would motivate employees to be cheerful, or that a dark room would prevent conversation and distractions and thus increase quality. In any case, Western Electric commissioned a series of studies to take place at the Hawthorne Works plant just outside of Chicago.

Three separate groups were analyzed from 1924 to 1927, each consisting of an entire room within the massive Hawthorne Works complex. Light levels were raised, lowered, and left the same, but there no difference in overall productivity. Obsessed with finding a way to increase output, Western Electric reached out to academia for support.

Elton Mayo, a professor at Harvard Business School, was tapped to lead the research team. At first, Mayo and his colleagues expected the process to be a relatively straightforward experiment that would involve various workers and simple factors reviewed over the course of the year. Instead of trying to analyze an entire factory floor, they recruited a small group of participants and placed them into a separate test room. This decision ended up stretching the project to a full five years and produced results that were completely unexpected.

In any experiment, researchers modify parameters called *variables* to try to influence the outcome of a trial. The Hawthorne studies tried an incredible array of variables. Experimenters added "rest periods" to the work, gave workers food during breaks and adjusted the length of the day. They even tried changing the compensation model to pay the entire group based on output. Virtually every experiment had the same result: *increased* productivity.

Here's the amazing part about the Hawthorne project. It didn't matter if the experiment was positive or negative. Give workers breaks, and they get more done. Take them away, and they get more done! Shorten the day, and output increased. Return it to the usual length of time, and output increased *again*. It seemed like any change would have a beneficial result. This did not make sense.

For decades, scientists have argued over what actually happened at the Hawthorne Works. Some feel that the experiments were poorly designed or the data was improperly collected. But most agree that the study gave rise to a phenomenon now called the Hawthorne Effect: people improve their behavior simply in response to their awareness of being studied, not necessarily because the variable has any real impact. By actually talking to workers, interviewing them, seeing what they wanted and changing parts of their work environment, the researchers inspired them to work harder and smarter.

The Hawthorne experiments helped to create an entire field of study called the Human Relations Movement. This was an organized effort to attempt to understand workplace dynamics based on the unique needs of people instead of treating workers as interchangeable parts. The improvement came not just from becoming meticulous but from recognizing that outcomes are tied to more than just environmental factors.

If the Hawthorne Effect predicts that our performance improves when we know *others* are studying us, we can be comfortable that self-reflection on our own work will likely be positive. This *metawork*, however, shouldn't be limited to people analyzing themselves. Reviewing, understanding and even pursuing opportunities within the interplay of success and failure isn't just one person's job. Improvement is the duty of the organization as well as the individual. The challenge is to forge a partnership that recognizes doing better also requires doing worse.

Business doesn't just need a methodology for success but a methodology for failure. People learn to walk by stumbling, and we should neither punish employees nor admonish management for making mistakes which are intended to lead to success.

Corporations and individuals both innovate by making, surviving and correcting bad decisions. Error may be critical to profits, but not every company is willing to embrace their mistakes.

Some organizations have a culture where failure is acceptable. John Kessler, an engineer with Honda Performance Development notes that "Failure is a by-product of pushing the envelope. When you fail, it's not necessarily looked at as a bad thing as long as you learn from it and make something positive out of it."

Still, this is not a true methodology for failure, just an environment that happens to understand that failure is part of the process. To see a field in which failure is aggressively and intentionally pursued, we can look at a small corner of the software development industry often called *extreme programming*.

Historically, most computer programs are made in a linear sequence similar to other complex engineering projects. First, the team gathers requirements, then develops a budget, designs an overall architecture and produces detailed specification documents. Next, programmers build out the new software product and then it is sent for testing. Finally, the program is approved and sent out to customers.

However, many software developers have long recognized that this model does not make sense. Unlike building a house, you can adjust parts of a program without having to tear down and start over. But most importantly, software is not just machinery, but machinery *made out of information*. That means that software engineers can readily build their own tool kits out of more software.

The extreme programming movement—also called agile software development—has taken a profoundly different approach. Instead of trying to create software that works, they start by creating software that doesn't work. This is a methodology called TDD: test-driven development.

According to the TDD philosophy, you don't start your day working on some small aspect of the software product. Instead, you write a small program called a *test*, which is designed to check the validity of the piece of the software product you are going to write later. In other words, you begin the entire process of development by creating tests you are *certain* will fail.

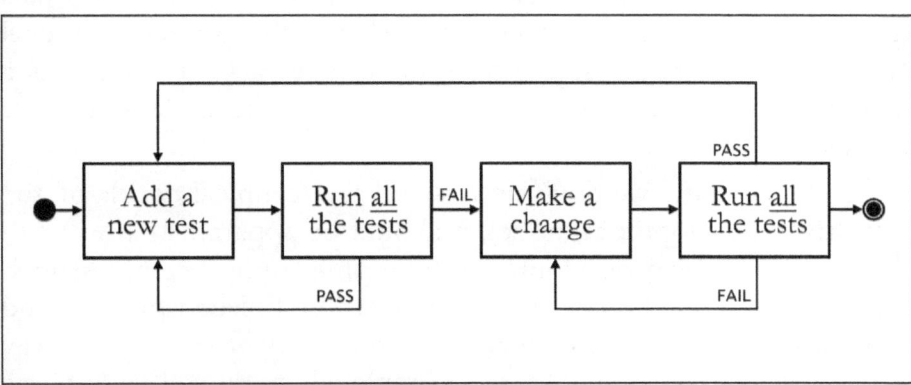

Test-Driven Development Activity Diagram

Test-driven development advocates state that every software application should begin not as a lofty specification, but as a series of failed tests. There may be thousands of these tests, checking tiny aspects of functionality such as "does the program allow the user to quit without prompting them to save?" or "does the tab key move the cursor from the first name box to the last name box." Every test isn't just an opportunity to succeed, it's something designed to fail. The tests exist before the program does.

The entire premise of TDD is the value of failure. Each test is expected to fail at first just to prove the value of the code in the first place. Essayist Scott Ambler sums up the approach as follows:

If it's worth building, it's worth testing.

If it's not worth testing, why are you wasting your time working on it?

It's hard to visualize TDD because most other testing systems are not built using the same technology as the product itself. Software tests are created as more software. If software fails during a test, the programmer just reloads the program. A civil engineer can't test the strength of his bridge each time he adds a new piece, because a collapsed bridge means he must start over from scratch.

But even if we don't understand the technical details of the test driven development model, it should be apparent that in truth this is *failure*-driven development. The philosophy begins through creating components that are not part of the finished product and will fail when first used. However, these failures help guide the way to success and ensure that the completed work will be of the highest possible quality.

Virtually every methodology for success includes failure. In order for a world class restaurant like Le Bernadin to make consistently amazing sauce, they need to bring the abomination of processed cheese into their kitchen. This insight comes from doing more than just working but actually thinking consciously about work. The *metawork* leads to recognition of the role of failure and the path toward success.

Ironically, the journey from doing it wrong to doing it right is filled with tools and signposts that are actually not all that useful. Sometimes, the advice of others, company traditions or advanced technologies actually waste our time instead of helping us out. This phenomenon is called the *productivity paradox*. We've all had moments in our lives in which complicated systems seem to be working against us more than for us.

Differences in individual success are not always caused by the tools we use. They are also caused by variations in expertise. No one can be a specialist in every field, of course, but an employee's satisfaction and productivity are instantly shortchanged when they are asked to do a job which they are not fully qualified to complete. The resulting work of this *countercompetent* individual will take longer and not be performed at the appropriate level. It's good to learn by doing, but we must understand that the journey from novice to expert winds through a place where our results are painful and arduous.

Perhaps the most significant aspect of the modern study of expertise is the Dunning-Kruger Effect. Science has demonstrated that we tend to dismiss the information provided by genuine masters and that true experts incorrectly doubt their own abilities. This reality is further reinforced by the fact that so many of us today are *knowledge workers*. Our jobs are based on acquiring, utilizing, interpreting and generating information. Making valid judgments about the quality of data from others is a crucial component of how we work.

This environment is a world away from our ancestors as well as those in the working class. However, there is a key connection between traditional laborers and office professionals: the psychological impact of visible scientific analysis. Taking an interest in the process of work tends to lead to a positive result because people respond well to direct engagement. Having a methodology of *any kind* with *any desired results* usually provides new insights, so long as employees know other people are fascinated by their work. The Hawthorne Effect teaches us a significant lesson about what happens when we're prepared to look at work under a microscope—we find out more about the people doing the work and what drives them to fail or succeed.

Despite the tremendous evidence that organized methodologies are effective and that embracing failure can produce stunning results, it seems like most workplaces are not open to either one. The test-driven development approach championed by a small corner of the software development movement is like a ship charting its own course far away from the rest of the fleet. This is a methodology devoted to *failing on purpose* by building out extensive test cases that show in great detail that the product *does not work*. TDD is the ultimate example of a painstaking approach that proves failure is the secret to success.

We all feel the pull to get organized at work, to develop patterns and systems for working smarter and getting more done. But for these ideas to mature, we must be ready to pursue systems designed for failure as well as success. We must build our business around the idea that a procedure may lead us into uncharted territory, through treacherous waters and perhaps to discoveries we never imagined.

Chapter 6

Failure at Work: Great Failures in Business

When your company is in trouble, you might not be doing anything wrong in the traditional sense. The world has changed, and you must change with it.
—Purdy Crawford

When we think of great businesses, we think of brilliant successes, not stupendous failures. Most of us work, and most of us do so conscientiously with the goal of supporting our families and enjoying our lives. We try our best each day to stay competitive. The word "failure," it seems, is not in our vocabulary.

But the history of business is filled with failure. The stories are told in every MBA program in the world. However, there's far more to studying these mistakes than simply finding out what not to do. The false steps of great organizations can teach us how to consciously seek out failure, how to react when failure happens unexpectedly and how to use failure to make smarter choices. With this in mind, let's review some of the greatest failures in business.

The tale we expect to hear about business failures is the journey from adversity to triumph. The American Dream is one of rags to riches, from obscurity to fame. A company that manages to rise from the ashes easily earns our respect.

In the 1970s and 80s, two major corporations were locked in a battle to see who could earn the greatest market share among billions of consumers worldwide. Coca-Cola and PepsiCo both engaged in the so-called "Cola Wars." As their respective sales figures continued to grow, every year saw the release of bold new ad campaigns, new product lines and further efforts to dominate the market.

The Cola Wars have become such a part of our cultural tapestry that it's easy to rewind back through your mind to remember the history of this struggle. Perhaps the first notable move was the creation of the Pepsi Challenge, a blind taste test in which people were shown to prefer the taste of Pepsi over other products. Coke responded in several ways, but most memorably with the famous "Mean Joe Green" Super Bowl Commercial in 1979. A few years later, they followed with the launch of Diet Coke. Pepsi fired back by signing a deal for a new company spokesperson: music sensation Michael Jackson. Each year brought new volleys in this battle between the two great beverage empires.

However, by far the most famous incident in the Cola Wars took place in 1985. This was not a routine announcement of a new product in the lineup, a new sponsorship deal or a new celebrity pitchman. On April 23, Coca Cola tried the unthinkable: they told the world that the most popular soft drink would now be produced with a new formula.

It is difficult to imagine the scope of this statement, especially without understanding what was happening in the soft drink business in the 1980s. Coca-Cola still had the number one product ("Coke") and the number three product ("Diet Coke"), but every year their lead was slipping. Coke had dropped from dominating 60% of the market after World War II to under 25% by the time they decided to release a new formula. Their main competitor, Pepsi, had not only diversified into many different types of beverages, but they had also pulled ahead of Coke in the most coveted space: the supermarket. If there was ever a time to try something drastic, this was it.

However, it's essential to note that it's not as if Coke was about to go out of business. The previous week, their stock was at a record high: over twice what the value had been four short years before. Coke was also operating bottling plants in more states and countries than ever. Coke wasn't preparing to sink. Rather, they realized that if they didn't do *something*, they might lose the right to call themselves "America's most popular soft drink."

The marketing wizards in Atlanta didn't have a solution, but they knew the problem. In controlled taste tests, consumers chose Pepsi. It wasn't that Pepsi *tasted* better, just that it was a little sweeter than Coke. When you're trying a few sips of a beverage in front of a scientist wearing a lab coat, you pick the one that makes your tongue happier. Supposedly, if you ask people to drink a full serving, they generally prefer Coke. But in a *taste* test—where just one sip is enjoyed—Pepsi wins most of the time.

It takes years to develop a beverage, trial it with consumers and tweak it to be just right. But the Coca-Cola employees had to keep their plan entirely under wraps to avoid discovery. There was no way to survey people and find out how they would react "in theory" if Coca-Cola decided to change their formula. It was either go or no-go; launch or abort. There could be no middle ground.

Finally, the plan came to fruition. After maintaining the same, top secret recipe for ninety-nine years, Coca-Cola released "New" Coke on April 23, 1985. Facilities all over the country switched at the same time. Production of the old formula ended within the week. Their marketing and PR campaign was so widespread, that one research study claimed that 80% of all Americans were aware of the reformulation within 48 hours of the official announcement. The company was fully committed to the new version of their flagship product. Too bad soda lovers felt otherwise.

The backlash against the announcement was devastating. Although there was some initial support of the product, complaints quickly started to pour in to Coca-Cola headquarters. The company logged some 400,000 letters and phone calls attacking the change. Crowds booed the appearance of ads for the soda on the scoreboard at Houston's Astrodome stadium. A lobbying group was formed called the "Old Cola Drinkers of America" who attempted to file a class action lawsuit against Coca-Cola. There were even reports of protests in some parts of the South, where people would pour bottles out onto the street in defiance. Americans love Coca-Cola!

In the meantime, Pepsi was having a field day. They used the announcement that Coke was changing their formula to prove that they had won the Cola Wars. Pepsi took out a full-page ad in the *New York Times* proclaiming their victory and made a major show by giving every employee a day off to celebrate. They quickly produced a new television ad campaign in which someone trying Pepsi for the first time exclaims: "Now I know why Coke did it!"

By June, it was clear that the new version of Coke would not be a success. Usually, soft drink sales rise with the summer temperatures. But as domestic stocks of the old formula were depleted, the company saw their revenue from the new product start to flatten. Within three months of the launch, executives sheepishly announced they would revert back to the original formula. "Old" Coke would return alongside the "new" version under the name Coca-Cola Classic.

July 10, 1985 is day that will live forever in the annals of soda pop. It was important enough that ABC News anchor Peter Jennings actually interrupted regular daytime programming to share the breaking story. Senator David Pryor, speaking on the floor during a legislative session, described the reintroduction of Coke as "a meaningful moment in U.S. History." Outrage subsided quickly and the American people soon returned to their former appreciation of the frothy beverage.

New Coke remained on the shelves, and was eventually re-branded as Coca-Cola II. But it was Coca-Cola Classic that quickly became the real victor. By the end of 1985, the original formula had already taken the #1 spot again, outperforming both New Coke and Pepsi. Six months after the re-release of the original formula, Coke Classic sales figures were increasing at twice the rate of Pepsi's. The soft drink has been "America's favorite" ever since. Today, Coca-Cola is the largest beverage distribution system in the world and continues to enjoy popularity around the globe.

Some industry analysts predicted that New Coke would be a blunder from which no company could ever recover. And as foolish as it may seem in retrospect, the reality is that Coca-Cola rose from the ashes to become the leader in their industry. It was a risk they didn't have to take, but one that paid off in the end.

The stakes were quite different for Corning. Like Coca-Cola, this was an organization steeped in American history. Originally formed in 1851, the company provided manufactured goods for a variety of customers. They quickly became known as innovators in glassmaking. Corning was one of the most successful producers of glass envelopes, or bulbs, for Edison's incandescent lamp. They expanded this work to produce safety-glass and heat-resistant glass, eventually leading to the creation of Pyrex cookware in 1915. The company also produced glass for the United States Navy, for millions of televisions and even for the re-entry shields for America's missions into space.

However, the product for which Corning is best known in recent years is fiber optic cable. These long strands of spun glass allow data to be communicated using laser light instead of traditional electrical signals. Corning's leadership in fiber optic technology in the 1970s and 1980s powered the telecom industry, which in turn enabled the Internet revolution. At its highest point, on September 1, 2000, Corning was selling on the New York Stock Exchange at an amazing $113 per share. With virtually all of their business in fiber optic technology, it seemed like there was no stopping this juggernaut.

Unfortunately, a boom cannot last forever. A mere twelve months later, the price of Corning's stock had dropped to a tenth of what it once was. A company that was supposed to be celebrating its 150th anniversary was instead trying to figure out how to avoid filing bankruptcy.

Company CEO James R. Houghton believed that he could turn the business around. He called upon Joseph A. Miller Jr., executive vice-president and Chief Technology Officer to produce a comprehensive analysis of the past fifteen decades of successes and failures at Corning. Perhaps the leader hoped to rediscover a lost product idea or an untapped market. Perhaps something in all of those years of ingenuity could be leveraged to rescue them from utter demise. Or, maybe Miller would find a project that the company was already working on which could become their savior. One product floated to the surface. It was called the DNA microarray.

In order to understand the potential of this concept, one has to go back in time a few years to the beginning of the Human Genome Project. In the late 1980s, researchers predicted that the next wave in medical research would require a complete map of every one of the 20,000 genes present in the human body. Knowing the position of each gene in our DNA would allow scientists to more easily discover cures, create vaccines and improve the quality of life for everyone.

However, just having a map of the genes would not be that useful in itself. Although this information might tell you where to focus your efforts, in reality you still need to run each experiment 20,000 times to see how each gene is individually impacted. The ability to browse the genome is kind of like browsing the web: just because the connections are documented doesn't mean you know which parts contain the information you need.

So instead of using the complete human genome as a map, many scientists believed that you could build a tiny microchip which contained a sample of all 20,000 genes. Researchers would then be able to test their theories all at once, dramatically increasing productivity. Every genetic research lab in the world would want to have such an amazingly useful technology. Best of all for manufacturers like Corning, a DNA microarray is typically used only one time. Each new run of an experiment requires a new microarray—which means recurring revenue for the manufacturer.

By the year 2000, Corning had invested $100 million in the project. They had announced a partnership with Massachusetts Institute of Technology and it looked like they would be the first to market: just in time to match the working draft release of the Human Genome Project. But while Corning was trying to finish their design, a competitor named Affymetrix had managed to bring their own version to the marketplace. Corning had failed to involve customers early in the process, and with their losses in the telecom industry, they had to kill the project.

It might seem like this failure would spell the end of Corning. Some would say that the company that had spent so many years specializing in glass should never have gotten involved in biotechnology. But Houghton, Miller and the rest of the team would not give up. Although the experience with the microarray had ended in failure, it produced a piece of knowledge which fueled Corning to surge ahead. As Joseph A. Miller stated, "We had discovered the marketplace of drug discovery."

All of the effort to try and build a DNA microarray had taught Corning a great deal about the process of biological research. Their customers were so focused on results that they were willing to purchase tools which used up their samples as part of the experiment. In fact, the technique Corning was pushing with the DNA microarray not only exhausted the supply of genes for each test, it also destroyed the microarray device itself.

What if they could find a way to conduct biochemical analysis *without* using up the samples? It might not be possible at the genetic level, but perhaps at the cellular level. Usually, Corning had learned, drug discovery was done by using chemical markers or radioactive dyes on living cells to try and monitor the impact of a drug during a trial. But these additives corrupted the cells and made the experiments less efficient. Luckily, Corning had another product idea they had already abandoned which could be used to study cell behavior using light. The technology was called photonics. There might be a market for the lessons of the DNA microarray after all.

Corning's management had learned a great deal from their recent failure. Instead of engaging customers too late in the process, a total of eighteen different pharmaceutical companies tested their new photonic device before the launch. Corning's Epic System is the first high-throughput screening system designed exclusively for drug development. Instead of manually inspecting cell interaction under a microscope, the patented optical biosensors are able to track and report on biological responses at incredible speeds. Some of these patterns were previously undetectable by any technology.

Although Corning came to the market with this product before anyone else, they already had competitors. Lance Laing of SRU Biosystems notes that photonics are revolutionizing the drug discovery process. "When we are working with customers, they are pretty surprised that we can get a result within a few hours — they are used to spending months."

The presence of other companies on your tail is a sign you are on the right track. New innovations often come from finding the wrong path. The story of Corning proves, once again, that failure is the secret to success.

Back when Corning was a very young company, a group of people on the other side of the Atlantic were debating a project far more ambitious than a machine for drug discovery. The group was called the Geographical Society, and was headed by a man named Ferdinand de Lesseps.

Born in 1805, Lesseps had an impressive career. He had served the government of France as diplomat in Tunisia, Spain, Portugal, Holland, Egypt and even the Vatican. Later in life he would be selected to formally present France's most famous gift to the United States: the Statue of Liberty. Ferdinand de Lesseps even made the long sea voyage to speak at the dedication ceremony.

But the reason Lesseps was the de facto leader of the Geographical Society was because of an achievement that had tremendous economic impact for France and the industrialized world. Lesseps was the driving force and primary administrator behind the Suez Canal project. The excavation of this 119-mile long waterway was an unprecedented engineering marvel. Some estimates claim that as many as 1.5 million different people from different countries worked on the project during the ten years of construction. The finished canal not only created a speedy connection between the Mediterranean and Indian Ocean, but made Ferdinand de Lesseps a famous and wealthy individual.

It was the success at Suez that catapulted Lesseps into the spotlight at the Geographical Society meeting in Paris. A commission had been researching the possibility of an even more ambitious canal project in Central America. Although many plans were presented to the group, only one person from the French delegation had any experience in working in the tropics. Lesseps had never been to Central America and bitterly ignored the suggestions of engineers. After all, he was the successful leader behind the Suez Canal. Thanks to his considerable political experience, Ferdinand de Lesseps was appointed President of the Panama Canal Company at 74 years of age. Little did he know the stupendous failures that lay ahead.

While organizations like Coca-Cola and Corning are known for offering a wide variety of products and services, the Panama Canal Company had just one objective: reduce long voyages by connecting two oceans. Ferdinand de Lesseps, trained as a diplomat and not an engineer, felt that his primary duty was to find investors. Lesseps was endlessly optimistic and aggressive. To inspire confidence in potential stockholders, he slashed budgets and cut time estimates without explanation. He quickly delegated administrative tasks to others, and hired the same contractor that had worked with him at Suez. After a brief trip to Panama and a lavish kickoff ceremony, Lesseps set out to visit the United States and Europe to find more capital for the project.

The failure of the French effort to build the Panama Canal was not a single crushing blow. Instead, the company suffered a long series of setbacks, mostly caused by overconfidence and lack of planning. Work was supposed to officially begin on January 1, 1880, followed by a few weeks of surveying to confirm that the plan was accurate. Yet delay after delay slowed the progress, and it took more than a year to assemble the necessary labor force, equipment and supplies needed in the remote area. Digging did not really start in earnest until March of 1881.

The course of this project seemed to include every misstep imaginable. The primary contractor on the project quit. Repeated turnover in management stalled operations. Accounting and planning errors led to wasteful surpluses and frustrating shortages.

Corrupt employees quietly sold company property and kept the profits. Foreign vendors provided faulty materials and labor had been difficult to recruit. Government officials connected with the project were embroiled in charges of bribery and malfeasance.

Not only were there business issues but Lesseps faced technical challenges as well. The French had planned a sea level passage which would require deep cuts into the earth, but the equipment was not large enough to handle the material. Mudslides occurred frequently due to poor planning. The hurried survey work had produced inaccurate maps and estimates. By the summer of 1885, the project was so far behind that crews had only managed to excavate one-tenth of the total amount of earth that needed to be removed. Finally, the realization of a major difference in tidal variation between the two oceans demonstrated that the overall design of a single straight canal—as Ferdinand de Lesseps had completed at Suez—would be infeasible.

The greatest tragedy in the French Panama Canal, however, was undoubtedly the needless loss of life. The first person to die of yellow fever was an engineer named Etienee, who passed in June of 1881. Some hospitals were constructed during the course of the project, but they could not begin to tackle the epidemics of yellow fever, malaria, and on-the-job injuries. No official records were kept, but most historians estimate the total death toll at around 22,000 souls.

It's hard to imagine how the Lesseps could have succeeded in finishing the Panama Canal after so many tremendous failures. The answer is: he didn't. The French Government had overseen several last-ditch efforts to save the project, including bankrupting the original corporation and forming a new one. They also pressured Lesseps to change the engineering plan to one that would use locks to raise and lower ships. It wasn't until 1888 that work on the totally new design was started. Unfortunately, these changes were implemented much too late.

At the end of the century, the French abandoned their project and made arrangements to sell the rights to the United States. Although there were certainly problems, the Americans largely began their canal construction efforts by studying the failures of the past. When John Frank Stevens came on as Chief Engineer for the project, he focused not on digging, but on making Panama a suitable place for an enormous human undertaking. Within six months after taking the job, Stevens had tripled the work force. Entire communities had been built to sustain them, including housing, mess halls, hotels, hospitals, churches, club houses and laundry facilities. At the peak, almost half of the 24,000-strong workforce was busy not moving dirt but *constructing buildings*.

Stevens also refused to be defeated by sickness. Chief Sanitary Officer Dr. William Crawford Gorgas believed strongly in the so-called "mosquito theory" about the spread of malaria and yellow fever. Supported by Stevens, Gorgas went on a crusade to fumigate homes, install screen doors, eliminate cesspools and provide clean running water. His efforts were a tremendous success. The last reported case of yellow fever in Panama occurred a mere eighteen months after Gorgas arrived in the country. Today, the Canal Zone is regarded as completely free of tropical diseases. Thousands of ships pass through the waterway every year without incident.

There are countless stories of failure in business. These range from massive construction projects like the Panama Canal to modest office buildings where the company can no longer afford the mortgage. Sometimes a long-standing organization like Corning becomes dangerously leveraged in one product and has to bet the company on something totally new. And industry giant Coca-Cola isn't the only beverage maker to experience challenges. Imagine for a moment what it would be like if the government decided to outlaw the very product your family business had produced for generations.

That's what happened to D.G. Yuengling and Son Brewery when the 18th Amendment was passed, which prohibited the sale of alcohol. But the management team did not close up shop. Instead they began to produce "Yuengling Special," "Yuengling Por-Tor" and "Yuengling Juvo." These were non-alcoholic "near-beers" the company brewed and sold for the thirteen years of Prohibition. This innovation, along with the proceeds from a dairy farm and several dance halls opened during the time, revived the company. Today Yuengling is not only the oldest American brewery but has vastly expanded their distribution into new markets.

We can go on and on with stories of failure in business:

- The Heinz corporation started out selling a huge variety of foodstuffs, such as Heinz Cooked Spaghetti (#23), Heinz Mock Turtle Soup (#14), Heinz Ripe Olives (#40), Heinz Peanut Butter (#22) and Heinz Evaporated Horsh Radish (#48). Most of those "57 varieties" of products didn't make much money or failed entirely—except for #42, Heinz Tomato Ketchup.

- In the fall of 1982, a madman secretly added poison to bottles of Tylenol in stores around Chicago, killing seven people. Although Johnson & Johnson had nothing to do with problem, the company took full responsibility, recalling 31 millions units of inventory and redesigning their packaging. Their response to someone else's failure has been heralded as among the top ten public relations success stories of all time.

- When the Japanese company Nissin Foods was facing financial crisis, they decided to enter into the American market. But almost nobody in the United States owned a *donburi* bowl for cooking and presenting their delicacies. Instead of quitting, Nissin adapted. They created a self-contained stryofoam container with freeze-dried ingredients called "Cup O' Noodles." The product took off and saved the business from near collapse.

- Speaking of fast food, Domino's pizza stinks. That's what company president Patrick Doyle effectively acknowledged in a massive ad campaign in early 2010. After airing customer reports that their crust "tastes like cardboard" and that their food is "boring and bland," Doyle led the company to reinvent the recipe from scratch. For Domino's, embracing failure and moving forward has been a major success.

Not all business failures have happy endings. The infamous Exxon Valdez crash that spilled millions of gallons of crude oil into Prince William Sound was widely considered an ecological disaster. By most accounts, the company mishandled the public relations and was practically forced to subsidize the cleanup efforts. A series of tire recalls in 1973, 1978 and 2000 were all downplayed by the manufacturers involved, even though the National Highway Traffic Safety Administration showed that the faulty products caused many deaths. Ford and Firestone pointed fingers at each other, and eventually cancelled all business contracts, ending a 100-year long partnership. And in 1996 the Coca-Cola Company introduced *Surge*, a direct competitor to Pepsi's *Mountain Dew*. The product failed, however, and by 2001 *Surge* was discontinued.

In the annals of business history, one can find screwups of all varieties. Yet in each of these cases, failure helped to shape the future of the company and sometimes the future of the world. The reaction to failure, the acceptance of failure and even the pursuit of an idea that many thought would fail helped to lay the groundwork for future success. With business, however, that victory may not come from within. It might just be a competitor who is ready to pick up the ball and run the moment you admit defeat.

There is a difference between the companies that failed and then succeeded and those that simply failed. Those who merely stumbled experienced failure, but did not have a mindset which allowed them to grow as a result from being knocked down. We must work *with* failure, not against it. We sometimes should even try to do things wrong. The ultimate question will be whether or not failure is merely a pattern or a part of a larger perspective on success.

Chapter 7

Failure is a Perspective, Not a Practice

> I think you can have moderate success by copying something else, but if you really want to knock it out of the park, you have to do something different and take chances.
> - Lee Ann Womack

Practice makes perfect, the expression assures us. If your goal is to be exact and flawless, it makes sense to attempt a performance over and over again until you've got it just right.

But failure isn't like other activities. It's true that we will fail. We can benefit from pursuing failure. But if we try to perfect failure, we tend to focus on the techniques for failure rather than the lessons we can learn. We don't fail for the sake of failure itself. We fail in order to succeed!

War is filled with failure. The very reason countries go to war is because they cannot resolve their differences through diplomacy. When war is waged, property is destroyed, funds are wasted and many people—both military and civilians—are hurt or killed. These losses are failures. They are failures endured in the hopes of a larger success.

During the latter half of the Second World War, the Allied forces were island-hopping their way toward the Empire of Japan. On many of these small land masses, Americans established bases and airstrips to facilitate the war effort. For the most part, these structures were temporary and would be abandoned or removed entirely once the conflict was over.

But in order to construct small airports on remote Pacific islands, the Allies needed to establish a positive relationship with the indigenous populations. Most of the tribes were fairly primitive and had no understanding of modern technology like artillery and airplanes, much less the massive military-industrial complex that made the entire operation possible. The natives simply enjoyed the huge cargo planes that landed and brought them all kinds of exotic items which they had never seen before.

When the war finally ended, the Americans cleared out and bid farewell to their hosts. Yet, at the time, what the U.S. didn't realize was that the islanders *missed* the regular cargo deliveries. They longed for the planes to return and were willing to try anything to bring them back.

Under the direction of their tribal leaders the local people began to slowly rebuild the infrastructure they remembered; however, since there were no canvas walls or metal supports, they constructed them out of available island materials. There were no headsets or radio equipment, so they fashioned models from sticks and leaves. With a religious fervor, they would act out sequences—ones which they believed would bring airplanes bearing wondrous gifts. The editor Norris Bird first recorded a Western name for these groups: "cargo cults."

Of course, the aircraft never came. After all, you cannot bring a cargo plane to a distant location by building a mock airport out of wood carvings. Tragically, though, many of the believers remained faithful long after these initial failed attempts. In fact, the BBC reported as recently as 2007 that cargo cultists still exist on the island of Vanuatu. To this day, people believe that if you build objects out of bamboo which merely *resemble* advanced technology they will magically provide the conveniences of modern life.

The notion of "cargo cultism" is common in many disciplines and its risks are easy to understand. No one would want to receive critical medical care from a couch potato whose sole credential was that he had watched every last episode of the television drama *ER*. There's a tremendous difference between merely copying what you've seen others do and actually understanding the concepts yourself.

In the pursuit of failure, the role of the phenomenon of cargo cultism is especially important. Just because someone else is trying a hare-brained scheme doesn't mean that it's a good idea. During the dot-com boom, a company called Beenz.com tried to create "Internet currency." When competitor Flooz.com arrived on the scene with their own form of web-based money, it seemed like the concept might have merit. Each company burned through millions in venture capital without earning a profit. The online news source CNET later highlighted both as among the most stupendous failures of the first Internet bubble.

Cargo cultism, therefore, is an extreme form of the Dunning-Kruger effect. Those researchers pointed out that we often make mistakes without even realizing the folly of our actions. The success of others is often dependent upon mechanisms which are not immediately apparent. That's why we need to catch ourselves when we see a skilled expert "make a difficult task look easy." The straightforward appearance is deceiving.

So how do we protect against cargo cultism? How do we ensure that we do not fail thoughtlessly, but instead understand our mistakes and recover quickly? A writer named Duncan Haughey argues that a key problem is simply blindly adhering to a methodology. In his article *Avoiding the Project Management Obstacle Course*, he writes:

> Project management by form filling is not an effective way of managing projects. These days many organizations and individuals whole project management strategy revolves around becoming slaves to a methodology.
>
> My worst experiences have been with organizations that stick blindly to the methodology regardless of whether it adds value. 'It says you fill in this form at this stage and we're jolly well going to fill it in.' Then the form invariably gets filed away and never looked at again.

Haughey's complaint is that if we are trying to manage any project simply by "completing the form" we are missing the point. Even if our *goal* is to fail—for example, to determine which approaches *do not work*—we should not just run through a predefined process without understanding it.

There is an essential difference between *failure without understanding* and *failure which creates possibilities*. To the outside observer, both may appear to be the same, and indeed have identical immediate results. But one is the realm of the cargo cultists and the other of the great innovators of all time. Good failure requires clear thinking.

Let's note that carefully: we don't need a plan to make a mistake. However, if we have a healthy perspective on what to do when things go wrong, it's okay to set out to fail. Our intentional error is part of a plan for eventual success. The combination of a positive attitude and an emphasis on understanding make intentional failure a worthwhile pursuit. As Peter McWilliams says, "To avoid situations in which you might make mistakes may be the biggest mistake of all."

In order to appreciate why we tend to view failure and success as an outcome of practice, we need to go back to where we first learned these fundamental concepts: our childhood. In school, we are taught to *emulate* the right answers. Although many great teachers strive to help students gain a profound and deep understanding of key concepts, much of our educational experience is rote memorization. There are some facts you just have to commit to your mind by studying them over and over again.

However, there are clearly issues with this approach to learning. In the late 1970s, scientists discovered a serious problem with the way we practice. The phenomenon was documented by John T. Bruer in his book *Schools for Thought: A Science of Learning in the Classroom*:

> [The researchers] analyzed children's performance on multi-digit subtraction in the course of developing a diagnostic program to help teachers identify and correct children's math errors. They found that multi-digit subtraction is "a virtually meaningless procedure" for most school-children, totally divorced from any understanding of the number system.
>
> After analyzing tens of thousands of arithmetic problems done by thousands of students [researchers] also found something else: Most teachers assume that children's

subtraction errors are random, careless, or the result of the child's not having mastered the subtraction procedure; the remedy is assigning more problems, urging the child to be more careful, or reteaching the entire procedure. But children's errors are not random; they are systematic...It's not that children can't follow procedures very well; rather, "students are remarkably competent procedure followers but ... often follow *the wrong procedures.*"

We need to highlight the logic in that last sentence: "Errors are not random; they are systematic." The reason children have trouble learning subtraction is not because they make unpredictable mistakes. Rather, children fumble in consistent, predictable ways.

For example, when computing **75 - 38 = ?**, many students will suggest that the answer is "43." They begin by comparing the first digit of each of the two numbers, and recall that 7-3 = 4. However, when a child tries to subtract the second digits (5-8 = ?), a problem may arise. Students might recall the factoid that "you can't take a bigger number from a smaller number," and will attempt to *repair* the problem by switching the two digits. 8-5 = 3, and thus the proposed result: 43.

When researchers demonstrated these issues to teachers, the educators rapidly acknowledged the issues and were able to change their curriculum to prevent students from developing incorrect procedures. However, explaining the discovery to schoolchildren resulted in an even more fundamental change to their self-image. They started to realize that they were not "bad at math" but rather, they were actually quite skilled at following patterns. Children's brains are able to act like mental computers, dutifully executing whatever programs have been provided. The study, in effect, shifted the blame from the "computer" to the "software" itself. As Bruer notes:

> What appeared before cognitive analysis to be careless or unintelligent behavior turns out after cognitive analysis to be sensible and intelligent, but buggy, behavior.

Like the cargo cults of the Micronesian islands, students in this research project were blindly following procedures handed down by authority figures. Because they did not really understand the relationship between the patterns and the desired results, they would often make mistakes without any comprehension of why the mistakes occurred. Students who say "I'm bad at math" are in some ways like cargo cultists who say "I am bad at summoning cargo planes." Both statements are demoralizing and inaccurate. The issue is not adherence to the procedure, but developing a perspective on the nature of the procedure itself.

Furthermore, the studies highlighted by Bruer demonstrate the Hawthorne Effect and the importance of human psychology in improving work. The students were always *competent* at following procedures, but once they received the new instructions they became more *confident* in their own mathematical ability. This shows the relationship between countercompetence and competence as well. Although the pupils were able to complete many of the problems before the study, they were inefficient and ineffective. When the teachers modified their curriculum, they not only increased classroom productivity but overall satisfaction.

Sixty years after the last cargo planes landed in Micronesia, cargo cultists still hold out for their return. Decades after scientists demonstrated that schoolchildren fail at math due to "buggy procedures," finding educators who consciously teach to prevent systematic, predictable errors is still challenging. As discussed in previous chapters on failure, we've seen how some unbelievably effective innovations will go largely ignored for centuries. Think of the cure for scurvy, which had to be rediscovered a half dozen times over hundreds of years before becoming an accepted fact. Human beings are great at following tradition, but even with overwhelming evidence we find it hard to put old ways aside for something new.

The road to perspective is often long and painful, and the life-and-death world of medicine is one where bad practice leads to tragedy. One physician, Dr. Atul Gawande, is determined to tackle this issue with profound ideas. In his 2009 bestseller, he talks about what may be the most important development in the war on failure:

> Here, then, is our situation at the start of the twenty-first century: We have accumulated stupendous know-how. We have put it in the hands of some of the most highly trained, highly skilled and hardworking people in our society. And with it, they have indeed accomplished extraordinary things. Nonetheless, that know-how is often unmanageable. Avoidable failures are common and persistent, not to mention demoralizing and frustrating, across many fields—from medicine to finance, business to government. And the reason is increasingly evident: the volume and complexity of what we know has exceeded our individual ability to deliver its benefits correctly, safely, or reliably. Knowledge has both saved us and burdened us.
>
> That means we need a different strategy for overcoming failure, one that builds on experience and takes advantage of the knowledge people have but somehow also makes up for inevitable human inadequacies. And there is such a strategy—though it will

seem almost ridiculous in its simplicity, maybe even crazy to those of us who have spent years carefully developing ever more advanced skills and technologies.

It is a checklist.

Gawande's book is called *The Checklist Manifesto: How to Get Things Right*. In the two-hundred page volume, he covers the role of this simple tool in medicine, reviewing its history, purpose, and incredible value. An especially powerful example is the role of hand washing. Everybody knows that medical professionals should constantly sanitize their hands, but countless patients die each year due to infection caused by overlooking this simple step. By empowering everyone in the hospital with a checklist that includes asking others if they have washed their hands, thousands of lives can be saved. Failure can be avoided if we're willing to admit that even trained experts can fail in embarrassingly simple ways.

The most interesting part of Gawande's book, however, is not that checklists work. Rather, the most fascinating aspect of these simple tools is that people are skeptical, even *offended* by the addition of a piece of paper to their workflow. They find documentation to be an insult to their expertise. After all, wouldn't most surgeons feel a little offended and patronized if a nurse with a clipboard asked them if they had scrubbed properly before entering the operating room?

Doctors aren't the only highly-skilled individuals to find a checklist revolting. In researching his book, Dr. Gawande discovered the story of similar instruments in other fields. Not surprisingly, checklists usually arise out of failure. That's what happened on October 30, 1935, at Wright Air Field in Dayton, Ohio. An airplane crashed and changed America's destiny.

The Boeing Model 299 was supposed to be a preordained champion. Expected to mop the floor against its competitors, it already had nearly twice the range of the other entries and could carry five times the payload capacity that the Army had requested. Not to mention, the Model 299 was fast—it boasted four engines and could outperform previous bombers. And though procedures at the time required that all manufacturers present a prototype for a test flight, the Army had already planned to order sixty five of the craft. Gawande reports that the flight competition was a "mere formality."

Yet when Model 299 rocketed into the sky it quickly stalled, turned sharply and tumbled to the earth. The fiery explosion killed two of the five crew, including Major Ployer P. Hill, the U.S. Army Air Corps' chief of flight testing. When investigators completed their report, they cited a peculiar, inexplicable cause of the accident: "pilot error." How could Major Hill, perhaps the best aviator of his day, make such a deadly mistake on a routine flight?

The answer was that the airplane was too complex. There were countless small details to remember. No matter how expert the pilot one person could not be expected to memorize every single component. Major Hill had forgotten to properly utilize a new feature of the aircraft which kept the rudder and elevator controls safely locked while the plane was stationery. Hence, the Army created the preflight checklist.

The luck of the Model 299 eventually turned around. Using the new document, test pilots flew the craft nearly two million miles without a single accident. Throughout the course of the next decade, the Army procured over 13,000 of the aircraft. They retired the temporary name of Model 299. Instead, the bomber was christened the B-17.

Not every organization, of course, has the power of the military to rapidly institute a new policy. The traditional method of flying airplanes, just like the traditional method of saving lives, left countless routine steps in the hands of the expert. That practice may often lead to failure. A popular quotation helps to illustrate the problem clearly:

> Insanity is doing the same thing, over and over again, but expecting different results.

Many claim that this was first uttered by Benjamin Franklin or Albert Einstein. But like the story of George Washington claiming he "could not tell a lie" after chopping down a cherry tree, neither of these individuals deserve credit. Instead, the first known appearance of this quote in print is a 1983 novel called *Sudden Death* by Rita Mae Brown. Repeating a false statement is another form of failure. When we tell the same lie over and over again—even though we do not know it's a lie—it is foolish to expect that unexamined lie to provide any new insight.

The notion of *failure as a practice* is fundamental to the study of failure. The cargo cultists believe that if they merely retrace the practices of others they will succeed in bringing planes to their tiny islands. The same is the case with bad business ideas that seem validated by the existence of competition, or project managers who blindly adhere to official company mandates. Students who do poorly on arithmetic problems are often following procedures as well, but such procedures happen to be a sequence of steps that produce the wrong result.

However, the development of *new* procedures often arises from something more than simply the practice of failure. When the Army's top airman crashes on a routine flight due to "pilot error," the new procedure *acknowledges* that one person should not be required to remember hundreds of steps in the pre-flight sequence. Likewise, Dr. Atul Gawande's campaign to encourage hand-washing consciously notes that medical professionals need to depend on each other to avoid simple mistakes in the intense, fast-paced environment of saving lives. Failure isn't just about practice, but also perspective.

Checklists aren't the only tool for transforming failure from the insanity of doing the same thing over and over into the brilliance of producing a new idea. Teachers in the study quoted by John T. Bruer were not given a simple checklist, but instead encouraged to redesign their curriculum. A checklist wouldn't help the cargo cultists in Micronesia, either. They don't need to perform their rituals more precisely. If they really want cargo planes to return, they will probably benefit most from comprehensive education and access to the rest of the world.

Finally, perspective means more than switching one failure for another. If you had falsely attributed that quotation about insanity to Albert Einstein before, memorizing the name Rita Mae Brown is not all that helpful. You're still likely to make the same kind of failure with another piece of trivia until you happen to come across a source that provides the truth. You may be practicing failure without even knowing.

Instead, we must develop failure as a perspective. When we cite a claim that "everyone knows" we may want to qualify our words. We should start to check up on facts and research for ourselves. Maybe what we know isn't actually true. Maybe what we're doing doesn't produce the results we want because we don't truly understand.

It is often good to fail. We sometimes need to fail over and over again to find a path to success. However, that failure cannot be blind repetition. We need to develop a healthy perspective on making mistakes. We should pursue failure with the goal of understanding the mechanism, not merely exercising a pattern. Through a deep knowledge of the nature of what we are doing wrong, we reach the possibility of learning to do things right.

Failure may be a powerful teacher, but it doesn't have an ego that requires acknowledgement. When James Joyce quips that "Mistakes are the portals of discovery," he is referring to a specific kind of error. These are the disasters that we actually recognize. The most tragic blunders are not the ones that destroy opportunity, but those that slip by unnoticed.

Definite failure helps clear the path toward success. Knowing that we have screwed up and understanding what we did wrong forms the foundation for changing our ways. The question then is what to do *after* failing. When we've succeeded in doing wrong and fully comprehend our mistakes, we are forced to accept that we've failed. Now we must choose where to go next in order to succeed.

Chapter 8

Congratulations, You've Failed! Now What?

> We can only make fantastic advances in technology through many failures.
> – Takeo Fukui, CEO of Honda

Just because failure is inevitable doesn't mean we know what to do next. If you choke on a word, you clear your throat and keep going. If you applied to a "safety school" then you will still have somewhere to go if you are rejected by the college of your dreams. If you're playing the "I've Failed" game with a group of comedy improvisers, the next step is to take a bow and receive your applause.

Often, however, we don't know what comes after we make a mistake. Failure might be upsetting, but it's often followed by an even more terrifying sensation: fear of the unknown. If failure wasn't on your radar, what are you supposed to do *now*?

The glib answer is that you try again. That's the advice of a Japanese proverb, *nanakorobi yaoki*, which literally means "[If you] fall down seven times, recover eight." The suggestion that we should persevere in the face of adversity is a little tired, to say the least. There has to be more to success than repeated attempts. We're supposed to benefit from our failures, not just rehash them over and over again.

According to Winston Churchill, "Success consists of going from failure to failure without loss of enthusiasm." Failure will undoubtedly be followed by more failure, but the right attitude is the first step in understanding the purpose of failure. Screwing up does have its advantages. Figuring out what to do *after* we fail is the path to avoiding that particular error in the future.

Let's begin the review of post-failure with the most obvious upside of making a mistake: **failure is educational**. If you get a bad grade on a pop-quiz, you can review the answers you missed to see where you need to study. Or if you're a teacher, you can look at the most-commonly missed questions on the last test to design upcoming lesson plans. There's a natural connection between failing and learning. Getting something wrong shows us where we need to learn more to get it right.

If you look back at the many of examples of failure in this book, you can see where each one creates a "teachable moment." The Mitchell Report, which identified an epidemic of steroid use in professional baseball, educated the world on the prevalence of drug use among these athletes and the relatively poor enforcement of the rules. If you cut yourself shaving, however, the opportunity to learn is confined to you. The experience is a reminder that razors are sharp and unless you're careful, you can end up with a small wound.

Sometimes the educational nature of failure creates categories of lessons. The recent tragic collapse of the I-35W bridge in Minneapolis, Minnesota can be thought of as four different individual mistakes leading to at least four different opportunities to learn. The design problem with the bridge suggests that perhaps engineers should reassess their methods for building bridges. The maintenance failure indicates that the procedures used to keep structures in good order need review. The inspection failure implies that either experts should visit bridges more often or that their inspection process ought to be more rigorous. Finally the usage failure shows that crews need to be more conscientious about the amount of weight they are loading onto a bridge.

Failure often educates us by showing us what must be done. When Michael Jordan lost his bid at the high school basketball team, he realized he needed to begin a daily practice regimen in order to become competitive. When Abraham Lincoln lost his first true love, Ann Rutledge, he eventually decided that he would need to move past his depression and begin a new life. When Warner Bros. half-heartedly made their first significant film to use audio, *Don Juan*, they never recovered production costs. The owners realized that they would need to fully embrace the new technology if they hoped to survive the cutthroat world of Hollywood. Failure offers us lessons that we often cannot learn through any other teacher.

If failure is a great educator, it's also a great motivator. **Failure provides opportunity for growth**. You can be assured that Michael Jordan is a better athlete having practiced harder than before and that civil engineers have redoubled their efforts to design, build and maintain safer bridges. Certainly, if we learn from our failures we may be inspired to change in the future.

A particularly fascinating example of the connection between failure and growth is the story of a man named Wasfi Hijab. He was born in Palestine in 1919 and attended the American University in Beirut. Hijab graduated in 1940 with high honors in mathematics, and during World War II he taught in a school in Jerusalem. When the war ended, Hijab was awarded a full scholarship to Cambridge University. He was to study under perhaps the most important philosopher of the 20th century, Ludwig Wittgenstein.

The experience of working with the master left Hijab dumbfounded. Wittgenstein's clarity of thought shattered the young man. Biographers David Edmonds and John Eidinow note that Hijab later reported the interactions "destroyed his intellectual foundations, his religious faith and his powers of abstract thought." Within only a few years of arriving at Cambridge, Wasfi Hijab left without completing his PhD and vowed to abandon the study of philosophy.

From that point forward, Hijab attempted a return to mathematics and normalcy. He married, raised five children, and spent much of his time in the United States. However, those short few months at Cambridge in the presence of the great man still kept him awake at night. He was supposed to be a mathematician, but thoughts of Wittgenstein's worldview had taken hold of his mind. Hijab claimed he was "over-exposed" the genius of his teacher, and needed a lifetime to recover.

Finally, in 1999, the long-time student crashed a conference in Austria devoted to Wittgenstein. He was not invited, nor even known by the philosophy community. Hijab's ideas were so powerful and his spirit so intense, however, that organizers provided two extra sessions for him to present. He was even mentioned in a write-up in a prestigious academic journal.

Wasfi Hijab needed *fifty years* to recover from his failure. Before his death in 2004, the academic became among the most prolific contributors to the study of Wittgenstein's ideas. Failure provides an opportunity for growth. Sometimes it takes a lifetime for that change to take hold and lead to success.

When we foul up, we learn lessons. We often realize what we can do to grow. Sometimes, however, what failure is trying to teach us is not so obvious. In these cases, we must allow our **failure to fuel creativity**.

That's what happened to the crew of the ill-fated Apollo 13 mission. As part of a routine procedure to stir the oxygen tanks, faulty wiring caused an explosion in the #2 canister. The shockwave affected the entire craft and damaged the #1 tank as well. Within a few hours, all of the oxygen from the service module would be lost.

The crew sealed themselves inside the lunar module—which they called the "lifeboat"—as they worked with Mission Control to solve the problem. There was plenty of oxygen available in this section of the craft, but not enough of the cylindrical lithium hydroxide canisters used to scrub the carbon dioxide out of the air. This was by design, because the lunar module was only intended to be used for a few days for the actual moon landing.

There were plenty of canisters back in the command module, but they were intended to interface with the oxygen system that had been inadvertently destroyed. Worse, these canisters were rectangular in shape. The astronauts literally had to find a way to put a square peg into a round hole.

The genius came from a crew back at Mission Control. Using materials they knew would be on the shuttle, NASA engineers assembled an unlikely contraption out of a sock, a plastic bag, the cover of a flight manual and lots of duct tape. Once they were able to test the jury-rigged device on the ground, the team provided exact instructions to the astronauts. They were able to adapt the square canisters for the round sockets and eventually returned safely to earth.

While the Apollo astronauts dealt with issues thousands of miles above the Earth, a 16-year old kid named Dick Fosbury faced another problem related to staying airborne. He was a high school athlete with a mediocre record. Fosbury's challenge was the high jump. He loved the event, but couldn't master any of the standard techniques and was unable to be competitive.

Then, during one practice, something happened completely out of intuition. Fosbury took his final strides toward the bar, and then twisted his body around in mid-air to sail over the beam with his back to the ground. The move looked awkward and strange to those watching, but it worked. Nothing in the rule book prohibited this approach. With practice, Dick Fosbury started winning competitions with his unusual high jump technique.

Nobody paid much attention to the young man, even when he made the trials for the 1968 Olympic Games. Fosbury managed to squeeze into third place behind his two American teammates and was not considered a favorite. However, when he advanced to the final rounds, people began to take notice. In a stadium in Mexico City, 80,000 spectators watched in near silence as the 21-year-old American made some warm-up jumps. Dick Fosbury was the only competitor to utilize the bizarre technique, and one of the only people in the world to defy the traditional approaches to the high jump. When he cleared 7 feet, 4 ¼ inches, the crowd went wild. That was the jump that earned Dick Fosbury a gold medal and set a new world record.

Not surprisingly, the so called "Fosbury Flop" quickly became the standard. Within a decade, it was used by virtually every elite high-jumper. Since 1980, everyone who set a new world record in the event did so using Fosbury's technique.

There's one more key lesson from failure beyond the opportunity for growth and the inspiration for creativity. **Failure leads to review**. After getting beat by Dick Fosbury and his weird methodology, countless athletes decided to rethink their own approach to the high jump contest. Once the crew of Apollo 13 had returned safely to earth, NASA launched a massive investigation to determine the cause of the explosion. This review in turn led to new procedures and changes in system design. When Wasfi Hijab finally recovered from his "overexposure" to Ludwig Wittgenstein, he began studying philosophy again and became a noted scholar in the field. When we accept that we've failed, it's hard *not* to look back and see what we did wrong.

Review is such an essential part of the post-failure process that we have already seen it many times. Remember James O. Clephane, the court reporter with a knack for breaking typewriter prototypes? He proved each successive design was a failure, but he also provided a path for the inventors to review their mistakes and refine the next version. Or think of the comments of racer Danica Patrick, who needed to review her first wreck so that she could learn to drive faster *without* crashing. Careful analysis of what went wrong is fundamental to these stories of improvement.

Of course, that investigation might happen on a much larger scale. James R. Houghton, the CEO of Corning, ordered a review of all of the failures and successes in the 150-year history of his company. John Frank Stevens, chief engineer on the American Panama Canal Project, spent much of his time studying the failures of the French. Whenever planes crash, bridges collapse, or epidemics strike, we follow up by trying to find out how the tragedy could have happened. The bigger the failure, the greater our efforts to review what went wrong.

Perhaps there is no cleaner example of how failure leads to further examination than the case of test-driven development. This methodology of computer programming, after all, requires first producing small tests of the software that the designer *knows* will fail. Then, the programmer reviews why the problem occurred and writes code which attempts to pass the test. Fixing bugs requires understanding the parts of the program that are incorrect. Failure leads directly to review, and review lights the way toward success.

Failure automatically brings us to a place where we have the opportunity to grow, where we can be moved to be creative, and where we feel inspired to review what went wrong. However, those natural aftereffects of making mistakes merely set the groundwork for the choices we need to make next. In order to decide what to do post-failure, we must interpret the *meaning* of our error. In the cycle of ups and downs in life, each failure has a specific purpose. If we want to benefit from our failures, we must learn to read the signs before us.

The most evident knowledge we can gain from mistakes is that **failure narrows the field**. Remember Thomas Edison's long struggle in his quest to find a workable filament for the electric lamp? Edison even refused to use the word "failure," telling reporters that he had "successfully found 10,000 ways that will not work."

There's something to that suggestion of changing the language we use to describe our experience. It might seem a little transparent to swap out a phrase like "making a wrong turn" for "using the process of elimination." However, if you pay attention to the terminology used by leaders, you will quickly notice the prevalence of euphemisms for failure. These are ways to soften the impact of failure while still focusing on the opportunity for improvement.

Listen carefully to a news broadcast or a conversation at work. Politicians talk about "trying a different tack" or presenting a "variation on the same theme." Expert problem solvers use words like "troubleshooting" or "eliminating variables." You're more likely to hear statements such as "take an alternate route," "go around," or "do an end-run" than you are to learn the story of why the direct approach did not succeed. The suggestion that "failure narrows the field" is a kinder version of "with enough boneheaded mistakes, anything is possible." Using the right language can help us to pursue failure more effectively.

There are many examples where failure merely provides an opportunity to refocus. A student who is struggling in his college classes might need to pick a new major. A suitor who asks for a date but is rejected might consider trying one of the "other fish in the sea." Many sports feature an elimination tournament, in which individual losses help to identify the best overall competitors. Even the world's most famous detective actively uses this kind of failure to solve cases. According to Sherlock Holmes, "When you have eliminated the impossible, whatever remains, however improbable, must be the truth."

Those words had not yet appeared in print when a young man named Francis Guthrie, a student at University College London, made a surprising discovery. When attempting to color a map of the counties of England, Guthrie noted that only four distinct colors were needed to ensure that no two adjacent regions had the same hue. He passed the question on to his old mathematics professor, Augustus De Morgan, sometime in 1832. Guthrie probably expected a quick answer from the master on what seemed like a relatively easy problem.

However, De Morgan could not solve the riddle. He handed it off to an American mathematician, Charles Pierce, who battled the idea for over a decade. The esteemed Arthur Cayley then worked on the problem in the late 1870s. He too, gave up and instead wrote a well-received paper on his attempts.

In 1879, Alfred Kempe distributed a proof which was widely applauded. The following year, Peter Guthrie Tait published an alternate method for showing that maps require only four colors. It seemed like the issue was resolved and mathematicians could turn their attention to other matters.

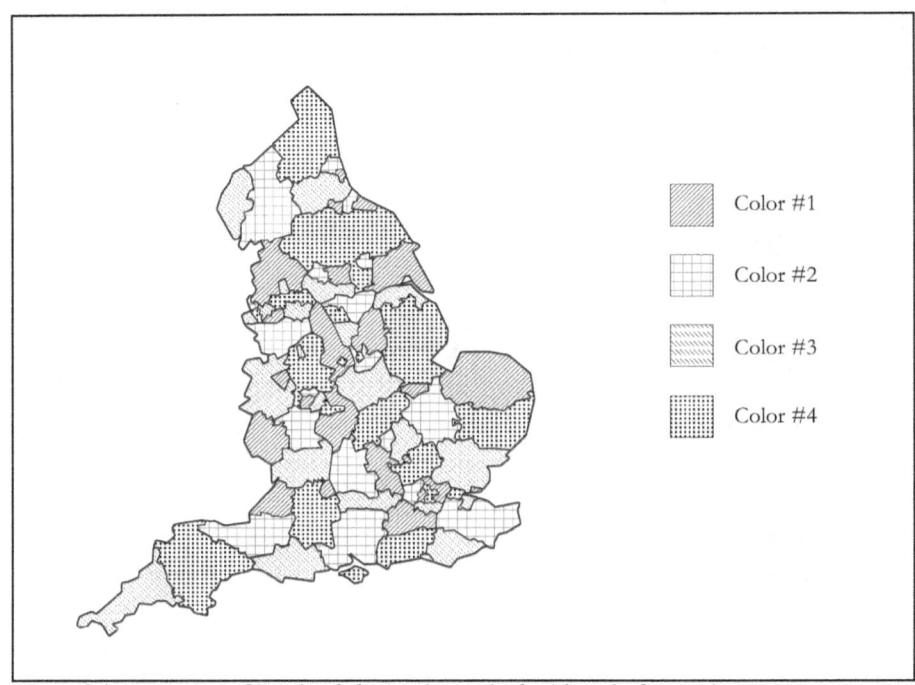

Map of the counties of England distinctly marked with only four colors

Just over a decade later, however, people began to question these claims. Kempe's logic was dismantled by Percy Heawood in 1890. Tait's proof was demonstrated to be incorrect in 1891 by Julius Petersen. Although the four color map problem was easy to define, it seemed to be maddeningly difficult to defeat.

As the 19th century was replaced by the 20th, more and more people began to work on this enigma. This included publications by Weinicke in 1904, Veblen in 1912, Franklin in 1922, Reynolds in 1926 and Winn in 1940. Each of these efforts helped to reduce the problem in some way, by eliminating false lines of thinking or showing broader examples. Even Percy Heawood, who had disproved Kempe's original claims, spent virtually his career on this one puzzle. His work on the four color map problem spanned over six decades, ending with his death in 1955.

By this point, the search for a proof about coloring maps was driving mathematicians crazy. The problem was well over 100 years old, and countless experts all over the world were racing to find a solution. Whoever finally cracked the case would certainly go down in the history books.

Years passed without a victory. In 1976, two researchers named Kenneth Appel and Wolfgang Haken invented a new approach. Perhaps inspired by the past century of collaborative elimination, they reasoned that that there had to be a theoretical number of *distinct* possible maps. Designs with only minor variations could be considered as mathematically equivalent. With every imaginable configuration drawn out, one could then patiently try to color each map to prove that it only required four colors. The only problem was that Appel and Haken's analysis showed the total number of irreducible designs at 1,936 maps.

Producing each of these designs and the coloring them in would take far too much time. Unlike most of their predecessors, however, these professors had access to machines that were extremely fast at conducting boring computations. Instead of checking almost two thousand maps by hand, Appel and Haken made use of several weeks of dedicated time on university computers. The process of elimination for the four color map problem was finally complete.

It might seem a little unfair to characterize the efforts of so many mathematical geniuses as simply crossing items off a list. The reality is that research is much more than a series of attempts. Instead, we should recognize that **failure often means to dig deeper**. The next step after failing is sometimes to dive right back in and work even harder than before.

That's part of the back story of science fiction novelist Cory Doctorow. After graduating from a prestigious high school in Toronto, he was unable to find a steady path. Doctorow was admitted as University student and then later dropped out—four different times. He served briefly in a few volunteer roles and worked various jobs. He helped to start a software company in 1999, just before the dot-com bubble started to burst in March of the following year. Based on this biography, most people would not expect much from Cory Doctorow.

Most troubling of all, the young man failed in attempts to pursue his lifelong dream of becoming a science fiction writer. Perhaps his résumé or his lack of experience dissuaded potential literary agents, but in any case he was unable to successfully navigate the complex world of science fiction publishing. Unwilling to accept the failure, Cory Doctorow attacked the problem with renewed tenacity. In 2000, he helped to research and co-wrote *The Complete Idiot's Guide to Publishing Science Fiction.* The work catapulted his career, and he has since published five science fiction novels and over a dozen short stories. Today, Doctorow is a highly regarded author and speaks at conferences all over the world.

Many of the examples we've already covered are cases where failure led directly to more research into the problem at hand. That's the case with engineering disasters like the I-35W bridge collapse in Minneapolis or the Apollo 13 crisis. Both of those events were followed by thorough inquires into what went wrong.

A similar process occurred with the research documented by John T. Bruer with regard to "buggy arithmetic." To understand the reason students performed poorly on math tests, scientists had to analyze thousands of individual answers to find hidden patterns.

A less obvious case is the failures documented by Justin Kruger and David Dunning. Remember the so-called Dunning-Kruger effect, which explains why we so often come to inaccurate conclusions? It turns out that we tend to overestimate our knowledge and ability, so we think we know the answer when we actually don't! In order to recover from failure in fields where we are not experts, we must be especially careful to question our initial assumptions and go further into the abyss of the unknown.

Traveling into uncharted territory was the primary activity for William Wilberforce. As a progressive Member of Parliament in the late 18th and early 19th century, he was urged to tackle the question of slavery. However, the issue quickly became personal. Wilberforce felt compelled to take a stand against the practice on moral grounds.

At first, the effort looked hopeful. Wilberforce launched his campaign in 1787, and helped to establish the Society for Effecting the Abolition of the Slave Trade that same year. However, the initial enthusiasm for the caused began to fade. The French Revolution became a major distraction and by 1795, the Society had stopped meeting. Wilberforce continued his efforts, but suffered from a sustained illness. His closest friend and ally in Parliament, William Pitt, died in 1806. It appeared as if slavery would remain in the British Empire indefinitely.

Wilberforce and his allies eventually realized that their strategy of demonstrating the inhumanity of slavery was not working. In order to overcome this failure, they had to dig deeper into the issue. Why did Britain have slaves? What would happen if slavery were made illegal?

The answer to both questions dealt with economics. Slaves provided an inexpensive labor force, and if Britain lost access to this resource while other nations still permitted the practice, many believed England would not be able to remain competitive. By the time this realization occurred, Parliament was already managing a war against Napoleon. The path to ending slavery would be based not on morality but nationalism.

Wilberforce's allies quietly advanced legislation that would effectively make it illegal for British subjects to engage in slave trade that might benefit the French. Slavery itself was still acceptable, but the 1807 law prohibited the *transport* of enslaved individuals. The British Navy established the West Africa Squadron to police the high seas. Other nations also allowed inspection of their vessels—

perhaps out of fear of the British Empire or in support of efforts that would slow the French juggernaut. Within the year, even the United States abolished the intercontinental slave trade via an Act of Congress.

These changes did not end slavery instantly. Rather, they proved that the exchange of humans as property was not essential to ensuring the future of nations. It would be another twenty five years before the Slavery Abolition Act outlawed the ownership of other human beings. More activists would have to dig deeper to find success through moral imperative.

In their book *Trust Agents*, authors Chris Brogan and Julien Smith note that "Those who succeed tend to be the ones who allow themselves to fail." Letting failure occur is difficult, especially when your idea seems so right. Sometimes, **failure simply means the timing is wrong**.

The easiest place to find stories which connect failure and bad timing is the world of technology. Earlier, we reviewed the case of biomedical engineer Michelle Klein. It looked like she would be unable to conduct her work in microfluidics because she needed some expensive, complex machinery. If the date she was assigned to this project lined up with funding sources or delivery deadlines, she might have been able to avoid the frustration of failure.

Klein, if you recall, was able to solve her problem by using Shrinky Dinks. Children's toys and games may not always have a unexpected secondary application, but they often represent significant design and engineering challenges in themselves. When a programmer named Ken Demarest was working on a video game called *Wing Commander* he and his colleagues wrestled with a frustrating error from a third-party module. The bug did not affect game play, but whenever you quit the program it would display a disconcerting error message. With the release date looming, Demarest had to act fast.

Instead of redoubling his efforts to find the source of the problem, Demarest acknowledged that the real issue was the tone of the message. So, he hacked the source code of the third-party module to change the error message from "EMM386 Memory Manager Error   General Violation" to "Thank you for playing Wing Commander." It wasn't the right time to hunt down memory manager errors, but it *was* the right time to change the wording of the warning so the product could be shipped.

Many great advances in technology have failed to take hold in the marketplace because they were offered too soon. That's probably what happened when a team at Stanford Research Institute organized a public demonstration of their ongoing projects. Led by Dr. Douglas Englebart, the team showed off some amazing innovations in only ninety minutes. The features highlighted included hypertext, desktop shortcuts, and multi-user shared-screen collaboration with two users at different sites communicating over a network with an audio and video interface. That demo was also the first time anyone ever used a computer mouse. It took place on December 9, 1968.

Why do those ideas still seem like new technology over forty years later? Perhaps Englebart was "ahead of his time." Many of the episodes from the history of computing are similarly tragic. Jef Raskin, who is credited with starting the Macintosh project, left Apple Computer to start his own company. From 1984 onward, Information Appliance conducted some of the most cutting-edge work in computing but in relative obscurity. Pouring over Raskin's writings and research from the time is like reading about a future that seems impossible. He once noted that his company achieved a "nearly unique accomplishment...a piece of commercial general-purpose software in which no bugs were ever discovered."

Information Appliance released their most famous product in 1987. According to Jef Raskin, the project was completed in a manner that was totally unheard of in the industry: on time and on budget! Their offering was a small, modestly priced computer that would be licensed and produced by Canon USA Inc. The machine was called the Canon Cat, or simply the "Cat" for short.

Raskin and his team recognized that true innovation required being willing to set aside traditions. That's why the Cat did not have a "startup screen" like most computers of the time or even today. Whenever you shut down the machine, it saved the visual appearance of the monitor. When you turned it on again—whether hours, days or weeks later—it would show that screen as it was booting. Since research studies showed that people require about ten seconds to mentally prepare for a new task, the static image of your last screen gave the computer enough time to load the operating system and prepare to work. It was effectively an instant-on machine.

Another amazing feature of the Cat was its use of the 3.5" floppy drive. Today, if you want to use computer that belongs to a friend, you must deal with their unique preferences and settings. The Canon Cat, however, saved all *your* personalizations to the disk along with your data. To use another Cat as if it were your own, you simply inserted your disk and turn it on.

Unlike other computers, the Cat used a keyboard that was actually designed for text processing. Instead of "overloading" keys with multiple different functions or relying on the mouse, Raskin utilized dedicated buttons with clear titles like "Undo." Acknowledging that search was such an essential component of computing, Information Appliance added a pair of "Leap" keys below the spacebar. According to one source, these made finding text "fifty times faster" than was possible on the Macintosh.

With such incredible advancements, one would expect the Cat to be a tremendous success. Within six months, however, Canon had sold only 20,000 units and discontinued the product. Some analysts believe that the typewriter and computer divisions fought over the ownership of the Cat and the company president cancelled the project to teach them a lesson. Another theory is that Canon wanted to invest in a new company being started by Apple pioneer Steve Jobs, but a personal feud between Jobs and Jef Raskin led to the Cat's demise. The most compelling explanation, however, comes from Raskin himself in the book *Programmers at Work*:

> How in the world do you sell something that's different? That's the biggest problem. The world's not quite ready to believe.

If we fail to gain interest from those around us, it's easy to assume they are not yet ready for our ideas. Often, though, failure isn't just about timing. Sometimes, the true lesson of our mistakes is that **failure reveals a resistance to change**.

The difficulty of accepting new circumstances or new ways of thinking is something that plagues all of us. Being stubborn is part of our nature. Whether old or young, male or female, rich or poor we automatically expect life to be the same and any kind of change is hard to accept.

A particularly powerful example of how human beings deal with uncertainty was first documented by the researcher Jean Piaget. It's called the "A-not-B" error, and if you have access to an infant less than 10 months of age, you can try it yourself.

To see A-not-B in action, spend a few minutes repeatedly placing an attractive toy in a location within easy reach of the baby. If the child *watches* you hide the item in location A, they should retrieve it themselves. After a few trials, place the toy somewhere new—a location B. Make certain you pick a spot where the baby can see the item in plain view. Most of the time, the baby will still go to spot A to hunt for the prized possession. Even though infants are able to recognize objects, they become oddly confused about their whereabouts when the item is still visible but slightly relocated.

After about twelve months of age, babies start to wise up and head for the location marked B to find the treasured item. But for much of our young lives, humans fall victim to the A-not-B error. We can't find what we're looking for even though we see it placed somewhere else!

Luckily, we grow out of this phase. The phenomenon of looking for answers in the wrong place, however, may seem familiar. Have you ever hopped in the car to run a quick errand and found yourself "driving on autopilot" to the office? Or perhaps you've discovered you are the only one on a committee with your school, church or workplace who seems even remotely open to a different approach? We are often *intransigent* (unwilling to compromise) or *complacent* (uninterested in change). Rarely, it seems, are we willing to begin by considering alternate views.

Much of this resistance to change arises from fear. In her 2009 book *The Happiness Project*, Gretchen Rubin notes that there can be fun in failure. We often avoid taking risks because we fear what might happen will be sad or depressing even if the outcome is something others might call beneficial! This fear of failure is effectively a fear of becoming unhappy.

Rubin's work documents a year-long project to seek happiness. To better embrace change and the possibility of being more content, she jotted down several phrases to act as guiding principles. One of her mantras was the sentence "I will enjoy the fun of failure." It helped to quell her sense of dread about the future and accept the truth that change can actually be fun.

Change isn't always a riot, unfortunately. Remember the case study about Mark, the recent college graduate with the business degree? Mark made what he called "the biggest mistake of his career" by agreeing to try to fix a computer the first day on a new job. That was a change from his own expectations about the position. The request to conduct the work, however, came from a supervisor who resisted the idea of calling on a true expert.

Failure through resistance to change can be especially damaging because sometimes the status quo is still passable. Mark's countercompetence with computers ended up having *some* positive impact. An industry professional would have been able to address the IT needs far more quickly and effectively. Mark's error might have been saying "yes." His boss failed by assuming he didn't have to change his strategy of keeping work assignments inside the company.

One can see the relationship between failure and resistance to change in business, in our personal lives and throughout history. Even though segregation was officially ended in the United States in 1954, as recently as 2009 the *New York Times* reported on rural communities that support two racially distinct school dances. Though society has determined that "separate but equal" is a failed strategy, some towns are not able to adapt. This may seem like a dramatic and tragic error, yet it is still based on the everyday reality of failure as opposition to change.

Likewise, the many centuries in which the cause of scurvy repeatedly discovered, rejected and forgotten serve as a testament to our inability to accept new ideas. The work of Dr. Atul Gawande and others to promote checklists in medicine is met with stupefying resistance even though these simple documents are incredibly effective. Even for something as important as life and death, it is hard for human beings to consider new ways of thinking.

It's difficult to imagine what it's like to have such clear evidence of success be turned into failure by those around you. That's what happened to a Hungarian doctor named Ignaz Semmelweis. He spent much of his practice helping to deliver babies, but was frustrated by the high mortality rates among mothers and infant children. In 1847, Semmelweis discovered that if he washed his hands in chlorine between deliveries he could virtually eliminate fatal infections among his patients. His colleagues discarded the concept despite his repeated pleas. They later had him committed to a mental hospital for his ideas, where guards beat him to death.

Extreme actions seem common among cases where failure is connected with resistance to change. Fifteen years before Semmelweis discovered the effects of chlorine on sanitation a French pharmacist named P.F. Touery was desperate to promote his ideas regarding the treatment of poison. He too, was unable to garner much attention from colleagues. So, in a demonstration before the French Academy of Medicine, Touery swallowed ten times the lethal dose of strychnine followed by an equal amount of activated charcoal. He lived. Today, charcoal is a standard treatment for poisoning. Failure may mean resistance to change, and thus dramatic action may be needed to achieve success.

We're used to receiving congratulations for our successes, but not for our failures. That's probably because a victory is something others want to emulate. Perhaps we need to learn to offer awards, accolades and even send greeting cards for when people fail.

After all, failure is educational. Failure provides an unparalleled opportunity for growth. The difficult circumstances and cramped environment brought on by failure often inspires creativity. Failure, ultimately, is the best way to learn. Making mistakes should encourage us to review those mistakes in detail.

If failure is to lead to success, then we need to recognize where to go *after* we fail. If we do it wrong one way we know to no longer go down that path. Failure narrows the field of available options. Furthermore, failure may guide us to dig deeper into the problem at hand, working harder with more exotic methods than ever before. Failure also may simply be the result of bad timing, so changing the circumstances, dependencies and expectations could be the best next step. Finally, almost all failure represents resistance to change. Remember the quotation from Grace Hopper which began our study of failure: "The most dangerous phrase in the language is, "We've always done it this way.""

Knowing the benefits to failure and the reasons why failure occurs provides something more profound than countless anecdotes of errors. We can begin to recognize that winning *requires* failing. The highest levels of achievement can only be pursued if we're willing to suffer through the mistakes and missteps needed to discover the path to success. Errors are the landmarks on the route to victory.

Chapter 9

Winning by Failing

Plan to throw one away; you will anyhow.
– Fred Brooks

Failure is the secret to success. To do what is right, great or brilliant, we often have to first go down the wrong path, build a broken version or suffer from the embarrassment of our mistakes. Doing wrong leads to doing right. Winning starts with failing.

We began our study of failure by inverting the statement made by high school coaches everywhere. Instead of insisting that "failure is not an option" it's far more powerful to insist that **failure IS an option.** Stumbling, heading down the wrong path, going for broke and bailing out are all part of the reality of life. The presence of ejector seats in airplanes, emergency exits in buildings and backup generators in hospitals are not a sign of a lack of confidence. Rather, these choices express the understanding that failure can and does occur. The question is not about whether or not we're going to fail—it's about whether or not we're brave enough to face failure directly.

That question suggests that we may want to **try failing first**. Countless examples of the finest achievers from history have lives filled with screwups, mistakes and tragedies. These include presidents like Grant and Lincoln, athletes like Michael Jordan, as well as a cadre of explorers, scientists and inventors. The artist Pablo Picasso, the science fiction novelist Cory Doctorow and computing pioneers Steve Jobs, Bill Gates and Michael Dell all dropped out of school before becoming wildly successful. That doesn't mean that *you* should walk out of class. Rather, these facts merely prove that even the most significant of failures may help lead to a brighter future.

Advising people to fail might seem odd or misguided, but that's exactly what we do when we encourage novices. Think of a child learning to sing or play an instrument—their early performances are little more than controlled noise and thus are basically musical failures. The strategy for learning often begins by **giving yourself permission to fail**. Missing notes and playing out of tune is part of the process. **Making a mess** of the music encourages exploration and creativity, while acknowledging that there might be a cleaner, smoother way to play. **Ignoring the wisdom** of music teachers, if only for one practice session, might help to establish a direct experience in making a mistake that is more effective than any lesson. Lose your voice once due to dehydration, for example, and you're likely to never come close to making that mistake again.

Pursuing failure may also benefit from **avoiding recommended tools**. There are standard books of scales and exercises, but the earnest music student who purchases sheet music for a popular tune will almost certainly expand their horizons. Likewise, **operating out of order** and **failing to follow the norm** can be of tremendous value to someone learning an instrument. These techniques are the genesis of musical invention and innovation. Finally, there may be no motivator to practice more powerful than **telling a white lie**, such as "I've already learned that piece." Any strategy for failing on purpose, no matter how unusual, will help lay the groundwork for future success.

If a healthy perspective on mistakes is such a valuable commodity, it might seem prudent to have a **methodology for failure**. But screwing up isn't like getting it right. You can put together a precise recipe that will produce a tasty meal every time. How do you create a framework for disaster?

The secret lies in recognizing patterns about the nature of success and failure. Sometimes, a cheap, mass-produced cheese is needed in one of the finest restaurant kitchens in the world—because the waxy product provides a consistent (if disgusting) baseline. Such innovations arise from *thinking* actively about the work we do. This metawork often leads to a startling recognition of a productivity paradox. Many of the tools we use in order to be more efficient may actually have the opposite effect. On a larger scale, we may find ourselves completing tasks despite our clear lack of expertise in the area. This *countercompetence* is especially damaging because the general poor quality of our work is masked by an overall positive result. Psychologists have proven that our lack of understanding actually makes us think we're more capable than we actually are. This is the Dunning-Kruger effect, which helps demonstrate why it's so easy to fail in such startlingly consistent ways.

The stories of failure are not limited to individuals. **Hugely successful businesses are plagued by failure**. From Coca-Cola to Johnson & Johnson, there are countless examples of corporations dealing with tremendous blunders. Even world governments deal with colossal mistakes. The nation of France failed to build a canal in the tropics, which paved the way for the American project to succeed.

The chief lesson from the Panama Canal fiasco is not just about methods but points of view. Ferdinand de Lesseps spent his time on fundraising and promotion. John Frank Stevens studied the mistakes of the past and focused early efforts just on making Panama a habitable place for a major construction project. It's important to have a process for failure, but crucial to know that **perspective is more important than practice**. As David Schmaltz notes, "More evil than good has come from the notion that we should 'stick to the methodology.'" We must be diligent and embrace useful patterns, but smart enough to recognize when these systems aren't working. Had Lesseps identified this failing, he might have recognized the folly in attempting to build a sea-level canal in mountainous environment with major variations in ocean elevation.

Finally, we must acknowledge that **after failure comes recovery**. It's certainly clear that failure is educational and provides opportunity for growth. Every question you miss on a test is a chance to improve. In addition, failure also fuels creativity and inspires comprehensive review. Radical new designs and detailed, fact-finding inquiries are only possible through high levels of failure. The primarily lesson of failure is that failure itself cannot be ignored.

The process of recovery, however, means putting this new wisdom into action. Failure may narrow the field, like Thomas Edison steadily eliminating candidates for light bulb filaments. Failure may require digging deeper for alternate solutions, like William Wilberforce discovering a way to outlaw slavery through economics instead of morality. Failure may be a matter of timing, like Douglas Englebart's 1968 demonstration of computer mice, video conferencing and hypertext. Failure may be a mark not of the quality of an idea, but of our innate resistance to change as human beings. Too many failures become permanent due to lack of popularity. To effectively recover from our mistakes, we must learn why they occurred and what they actually mean.

Journalist Paul Brown, writing for *The New York Times*, notes that "Successful entrepreneurs invariably say that they have learned as much from their failures as their successes." Countless examples support this theory; from stumbling while learning to walk to crash testing cars in order make them safer. Even though we can understand the importance of failure, it's still hard to internalize embracing our mistakes.

Professors Amy C. Edmondson of Harvard University and Mark D. Cannon of Vanderbilt point out a psychological justification for ignoring our errors. They write that "Individuals experience negative emotions when examining their own failures, and this can chip away at self-confidence and self-esteem. Most people prefer to put past mistakes behind them rather than revisit and unpack them for greater understanding."

The researchers continue by noting that the foundation of our model for workplace and personal success is the *exact opposite* of what is actually needed. "Conducting an analysis of a failure requires a spirit of inquiry and openness, patience, and a tolerance for ambiguity...however, most managers admire and are rewarded for decisiveness, efficiency, and action rather than for deep reflection and painstaking analysis."

In simpler language, although failure is the secret to success, the structure of workplaces and society at large encourages us to avoid even *talking* about failure. Our default mindset is an enormous productivity paradox. The very key to improvement—embracing and reflecting upon failure—is a way of thinking we are prone to ignore.

We find this irony in every aspect of our lives. No one wants to hear about the classes where you struggled to earn a C, but the ones where you easily scored an A+. The answer to the greeting "how are you" is almost always some version of the word "fine." The standard interview question about our own weaknesses is a practically an invitation to spin a comment about "working too hard." We don't like to dwell on anything remotely negative. Yet, that's exactly what we must do if we want to achieve unprecedented success.

J.K. Rowling, author of the hugely popular *Harry Potter* series, was invited to give the commencement address at Harvard University in 2008. After selling millions of books and earning millions in royalties, one might expect her self-confidence to have shot through the roof. However, Rowling opened her address by admitting her nervousness. She told herself and the crowd that she would take deep breaths. The famous writer then went on to explain how her own commencement speaker had been a source of great inspiration, because Rowling couldn't remember a single word from that speech. "This liberating discovery," stated the famous author, "enables me to proceed without any fear that I might inadvertently influence you to abandon promising careers."

These remarks were not just introductory but set the tone for her entire presentation. Admitting weakness, personal failings and the ineffectual nature of past efforts seemed to calm the speaker and connect with those assembled. Her thesis was simple: "On this wonderful day when we are gathered together to celebrate your academic success, I have decided to talk to you about the benefits of failure."

Most commencement addresses are not about the glorious advantages of making painful mistakes. Most graduates go on to interviews where they try to leverage past success. Essayist and venture capitalist Paul Graham, however, wanted to know whether or not failure would be a valuable commodity. He called up hiring managers at Yahoo, Amazon, Microsoft, Cisco and Google to ask them how they would feel about two candidates who were identical in every regard except one. The difference between these two theoretical applicants is that one worked for two years for a big company, while the other helped create a startup that tanked. Every manager said they preferred the failure.

Most interviewees want to show off their impressive resume, but perhaps the interview process should be about our mistakes as much as our victories. This isn't just true for high tech careers but also those in sales. David Sandler, creator of the immensely popular Sandler Selling System, tops his list of 49 maxims with similar advice. "Rule #1: You have to learn to fail, to win."

Sandler isn't the only business guru who stresses failure. Richard Farson and Ralph Keys advance a similar concept in their book *Whoever Makes the Most Mistakes Wins: The Paradox of Innovation*. They propose a simple formula which puts the challenge of failure into sharp focus. "Not making mistakes = not trying hard enough." Failure requires real effort. The manual in your hands right now is a guidebook, but if you really want to get out there and screw things up you need to boldly pursue your own failures.

Even the book you are now reading was made possible due to a serious mistake. Ira Washington Rubel, the owner of a New Jersey print shop, must have felt like a complete idiot when he realized he did not correctly load paper into his rotary press. Therefore, the ink-soaked metal type did not press against a blank piece of stock, but rather "printed" on the rubber roller used to advance pages through the system.

Although Rubel probably expected a big mess of ink in his expensive machine, he later discovered that when the wheel came around again the rubber could actually transfer an image to the back side of the paper. Even more curiously, the reversed print was much crisper and more detailed than he had ever seen from a direct application of traditional block metal type. Apparently, the soft, malleable surface of the rubber better conformed to the paper. Soon, Ira Washington Rubel was designing a new mechanism. His boneheaded mistake of failing to use the rotary press correctly led to the invention of offset printing.

Likewise, in our consulting practice, we help companies recognize that improvement comes from trial and error, with the emphasis on failure. No system or approach, however ideal for the present moment, should be immune from analysis or reinvention. Rewards come from the presence of risks, risks come from taking chances, and the ability to take a chance arises when we are ready to embrace failure. Success comes directly from failure, not just in spite of it.

There is a story of two strangers who found themselves sharing a room in an long-term care unit in a hospital. The first man was older and had been diagnosed with a terminal disease. The younger of the two men was recovering from a serious car accident, and was almost completely immobile. Although their families visited as much as possible, the two men occasionally struck up a conversation with each other.

As the days became weeks, they talked about everything. They shared stories from their lives, discussed their jobs and debated philosophy and politics. With nothing else to do to escape their respective pain, the two men became close friends.

Once a day, the nurses came in and propped up the older gentlemen to allow the fluid to drain out of his lungs. During this time, he would take the opportunity to tell his friend about what he could see from the window. It was their only unfettered access to the outside world, and the young man in his cast relished this description like no other.

It turned out that this side of the hospital faced a park, and through the window the older man could see a pond with ducks and a wandering path. He painted a picture with words, laying out in exquisite detail everything that they could see. He talked about children playing the in park and feeding the birds, about people walking their dogs, about couples holding hands. The other man could not see any of this, of course, but he closed his eyes and imagined the scene.

One day a parade went down the street in front of the park, and the old man excitedly relayed everything he could. He talked about the uniforms of the marching bands and the beautiful, ornate floats that smoothly glided past. The younger man could not hear or see any of this from across the room, but he took great pleasure in imagining the scene.

Then, one morning, the nurses came into change the bedpans and check on their patients. They found that the older gentlemen had quietly passed in his sleep. The nurses removed his lifeless form and let his friend know the sad news.

It was expected, of course, but the young man still felt a great loss. He was growing stronger every day and was recovering his range of motion. He tried to embrace life and cherish the memory of his new friend. After a few more weeks, when it seemed appropriate, he asked the nurses if he could be moved to the other side of the room.

They conferred with the doctors and agreed. The nurses knew that the two men had become close over the months and quietly acknowledged among themselves that it would be meaningful for the accident victim to take the space occupied by his deceased friend. So they went through the laborious process of carefully moving him, with all of his slings, casts and various machines, to the space on the opposite side of the room.

Once he was comfortable, the nurses left. And when he was sure they were out of earshot, the young man forced himself to lean up in bed. He strained against the pain, gritting his teeth. With all his might, he propped himself up and turned his head.

There was no window. His bed was alongside a blank wall.

He looked around in confusion. Had he been moved to a different room? Was he somehow disoriented? Panicked, he called in the nurses to explain the situation. What would have compelled his roommate to describe all those beautiful scenes when there was nothing there?

The nurse shrugged. "Perhaps he just wanted to brighten your world."

The story of the two men is uplifting and inspirational. If you analyze it carefully, however, it is a tale of failure. It is about accidents and disease, about death and dying. It is a story of an incredibly intricate deception. So much of the value that one man holds in this friendship is based on an enormous fabrication. Yet at the same time, the telling offers a powerful message. Rebirth arises from struggle. Fact, meaning and progress come from falsehood, confusion and stagnation. Sometimes telling a lie is the only way to reveal a truth. Failure is the secret to success.

In the rotunda of the Administration Building which manages the Panama Canal, there is a plaque. It carries these famous words of President Theodore Roosevelt, among the strongest supporters of the great project:

> It is not the critic who counts, not the man who points out how the strong man stumbled, or where the doer of deeds could have done them better. The credit belongs to the man who is actually in the arena; whose face is marred by dust and sweat and blood; who strives valiantly, who errs and comes short again and again; who knows the great enthusiasms, the great devotions, and spends himself in a worthy cause; who, at the best, knows in the end the triumph of

high achievement; and who, at the worst, if he fails, at least fails while daring greatly, so that his place shall never be with those cold and timid souls who know neither victory nor defeat.

We would do well to be the men and women who are "actually in the arena." No greatness can be achieved without folly. No genius may be formed without foolishness. We must fail, boldly, proudly and with intent in order to succeed.

Action Office, 77
Advertising (poker), 62
American Dream, 96
A-not-B, 147
Apollo 13, 133, 135, 141
argumentum ad populum, 54
B-17, 123
Bell, Alexander Graham, 47, 64, 160
Berners-Lee, Tim, 40
Biggest Loser., 66
Bohr, Niels, 84
Bruer, John T., 117, 119, 125, 141
Brynjolfsson, Erik, 76
buggy arithmetic, 141
Canon Cat, 146
cargo cultism, 115, 116
cargo cults, 114, 119
Cartier, Jacques, 51
Checklist Manifesto, 121
Churchill, Winston, 130
Classroom, 117
Clephane, James O., 48, 49, 135
coffee housing (poker), 62
Cola Wars, 96, 98
Columbus, Christopher, 55, 56
competence, 78, 80, 119
Cook, Captain James, 52
Corning, 99, 101, 102, 104, 105, 106, 109, 135
countercompetence, 79, 83, 119, 149, 156
Dane Mitchell, 47
de Gama, Vasco, 51
de Lesseps, Ferdinand, 105
Densmore, James, 49
design problem, 131

DNA microarray, 101, 102, 104
Doctorow, Cory, 140, 141, 155
Don Juan, 37, 131
Drucker, Peter, 85
Dunning, David, 83, 84, 85, 93, 115, 141, 156
Dunning-Kruger effect,, 83, 141, 156
Edison, Thomas, 45, 100, 136, 157
Education, 86, 117
Emancipation Proclamation, 32
Englebart, Dr. Douglas, 145
Exxon Valdez, 110
Failcamp Philly, 14
FailCon 2009, 14
Failing on purpose, 43
Federal Highway Administration, 15
fiber optic cable, 101
Firestone, 111
Ford, 74, 111
Fosbury Flop, 134
Fosbury, Dick, 134, 135
four color map problem, 139, 140
Gawande, Dr. Atul, 120, 121, 122, 123, 124, 149
George Washington, 12, 13, 66, 124
Gone with the Wind, 40
Graham, Sylvester, 47, 64, 160
Grant, 28, 29, 155
Grant Ulysses S., 26, 28, 29
Green, Bob, 32
Guthrie, Francis, 137, 138
Happiness Project, 148
Haughey, Duncan, 116

Hawthorne Effect, 88, 93, 119
Heinz Tomato Ketchup, 109
Hijab, Wasfi, 132, 133, 135
Holmes, Sherlock, 137
Honda Performance
   Development, 89
Hopper. Grace, 11, 152
Human Relations Movement, 88
I-35W bridge, 16, 131, 141
improv, 44
incompetence, 78, 84
Information Appliance, 145, 146
inspection failure,, 18
Internet currency, 115
Johnson, Earvin, 33
Johnstone, Keith, 44
Jordan, Michael, 32, 33, 34, 35,
   36, 131, 155
Kessler, John, 89
Klein, Michelle, 58, 59, 144
knowledge workers, 85, 93
Kruger, Justin, 83, 84, 85, 93,
   115, 141
Lancaster, Captain James, 52
limey, 52
Lincoln, Abraham, 26, 29, 31,
   32, 131
Macy, Rowland Hussey, 40
magazine Failure, 15
maintenance failure, 16, 131
Mason Weems,, 13
metacognitive ability, 84
methodology, 75, 78, 80, 83, 85,
   88, 89, 90, 92, 93, 94, 116,
   135, 136, 156, 157
microfluidics, 58, 144
Midsummer Night's Dream, 39
Mitchell Report, 11, 12, 130
Model 299, 123

Moore, Gordon, 22
nanakorobi yaoki, 130
New Coke, 99
Nissin, 110
noble lie, 70
Panama Canal, 106, 107, 109,
   135, 157, 164
Patrick, Danica, 75, 110, 135
Pepsi Challenge, 96
Picasso, Pablo, 66, 67, 155
poker, 61
Probst, Robert, 77
productivity paradox., 76, 93,
   156, 158
QWERTY, 50
Remington Arms, 49
resistance to change, 147, 148,
   149, 151, 152, 157
Rin Tin Tin!, 37
Rutledge, Ann, 31, 131
scrollbar, 18, 19, 20, 21
scurvy, 51, 52, 53, 54, 120, 149
Sholes, Christopher Latham, 48,
   49, 50
Shrinky Dinks, 58, 59, 144
Slave Trade, 142
Space Jam, 36
Stevens, John Frank, 108, 135,
   157
Suez Canal, 105, 106
Surge, 111
TDD, test-driven development.,
   90, 91, 92, 94
teachable moment., 130
test-driven development, 90, 94,
   136
The Jazz Singer, 39
Todd, Mary, 31
Trust Agents, 144

Tylenol, 109
typesetting machine, 48
typewriter, 49, 135, 147
Ulrich, Laurel Thatcher Ulrich, 71, 72
usability, 15, 18, 20, 21, 22
usage failure, 18, 131
Vaught, Steve, 66
Vincent Van Gogh, 40

Waikato National Contemporary Art Award, 47
Warner Bros., 36, 37, 38, 39, 131
Warner, Sam, 37, 39
Where the North Begins, 37
white lies, 67, 68, 69, 71
Williams, Roy, 33
World Wide Web, 40
www.failuremag.com, 15
Yuengling, 109

www.ingramcontent.com/pod-product-compliance
Lightning Source LLC
Chambersburg PA
CBHW021418210526
45463CB00001B/423